Effective Supervision in Social Work

Effective Supervision in Social Work

KATE HOWE

IVAN GRAY

Series Editor: Keith Brown

Learning Matters
An imprint of SAGE Publications Ltd
1 Oliver's Yard
55 City Road
London EC1Y 1SP

SAGE Publications Inc.
2455 Teller Road
Thousand Oaks, California 91320

SAGE Publications India Pvt Ltd
B 1/I 1 Mohan Cooperative Industrial Area
Mathura Road
New Delhi 110 044

SAGE Publications Asia-Pacific Pte Ltd
3 Church Street
#10-04 Samsung Hub
Singapore 049483

Editor: Luke Block
Development editor: Lauren Simpson
Production controller: Chris Marke
Project management: Swales & Willis Ltd, Exeter, Devon
Marketing manager: Tamara Navaratnam
Cover design: Wendy Scott
Typeset by: Swales & Willis Ltd, Exeter, Devon

Library of Congress Control Number: 2012946927

British Library Cataloguing in Publication Data

A catalogue record for this book is available from the British Library

ISBN 978 1 44626 654 0
ISBN 978 1 44626 655 7 (pbk)

Contents

List of figures

List of tables

List of activities

Foreword

The social work profession has seen unprecedented public and media interest in recent years due, in part, to some well-publicised failings within the care system. However, what is often not reported are the countless stories of excellent practice, where social work professionals make a real and valuable contribution to the lives of vulnerable citizens.

This is not only a frequently thankless task but often an emotionally draining one, which demands great personal resource and commitment from the professional.

High quality supervision is key to supporting these front-line practitioners in order to help prevent burnout, to support reflective practice and to help professional development. Kate Howe and Ivan Gray have written this text as part of the Sage/Learning Matters leadership and management series in order to stimulate and support the best possible levels of supervision within the caring professions.

It is packed full of advice, information and guidance for all potential and active supervisors to help them reflect on, and develop, their supervision of the staff they supervise. This text forms the basis of our supervision and leadership unit here at the Centre for Post-Qualifying Social Work but will be of value to all engaged in this area of study or development, and I warmly commend it to all social work practitioners.

As always, the texts in this series are written to promote and support the best possible social work practice, with the aim that the users and carers of social work and care services receive the best possible support and service.

Professor Keith Brown
Director of the Centre for Post-Qualifying Social Work
Bournemouth University

About the authors

Kate Howe is a a senior lecturer in social work at Bournemouth University. She is a qualified social worker and has supervised and managed teams in the statutory and voluntary sector. Her research interests include conflict management and developing good leadership skills.

Ivan Gray holds academic and professional qualifications in social work and management and specialises in management development. Before his retirement this summer, he was pro-gramme leader for the BA in Health and Social Care Management and MA in Leading and Developing Services at Bournemouth University.

Introduction

'Supervision is the cornerstone of good social work practice and *should be seen to operate effectively at all levels of the organisation*' (Laming, 2003: 12).

The importance of supervision in good quality professional social work practice is very well accepted. Munro (2011a), the Social Work Reform Board (SWRB) (SWRB, 2011), and Skills for Care (2012a) have all confirmed its criticality and value. Its role in social work is quite unique in the caring services in that it usually combines management with professional supervision. Usually it is seen as central to service delivery; it is the lynchpin of good practice and practice development as well as being the way to monitor and ensure adherence to organisational policy and manage organisational performance and service quality.

Aims of the book

We have written this book because we believe that effective supervision is a complex and demanding activity requiring commitment and a high level of skill and knowledge. The current initiatives to improve the quality of supervision such as the Reform Board standards are crucial to the future of the profession, but they will not be successful on their own. For genuine progress to be made there needs to be changes made at many different levels. Training supervisors is important, but needs to be set in a context of organisational policies that support good practice. Empowering and upskilling individual supervisors will make a difference to the quality of supervision only as long as they are supported to prioritise this crucial part of their workload in a workplace that has stretched resources and increasing pressures.

We therefore aim to consider all aspects of supervision, including the personal effectiveness of the individual supervisor, the dynamics of the supervisory relationship and the organisational issues of implementing good supervision policies.

We also recognise that there is no single model of effective supervision, or any easy answers. Rather there are a range of perspectives from different traditions that might prove useful in helping a supervisor develop their practice. We aim to examine a number of these, taken from a variety of subject areas such as leadership and management theory, professional skills and knowledge, counselling and communications theory, in relationship to supervisory practice.

We will try and do justice to this complexity and accept that often what we are offering is tentative, inviting supervisors to consider perspectives and issues rather than offering them as proven. This is perhaps the essence of the book; it invites supervisors to engage in developing their own personal practice and ultimately it will be their response to this challenge that will determine the success or failure of current initiatives. Supervision has not been well researched, and without an evidence base sustained improvement will be dependent on this engagement and also on action learning and experimentation by supervisors to develop their practice and the organisation. Our aim and hope is that the particular approach of this book might make a small contribution to improvement initiatives, helping tip the balance towards good quality supervisory practice.

Who is the book for?

This book is primarily for first line managers who supervise a team of social workers and is designed to offer a broad range of perspectives and models they can draw on. It seeks to draw together contemporary knowledge and understanding and to address, with what is available, current challenges and problems. Given the centrality of supervision to professional social work practice it is also very relevant for:

- senior practitioners;
- health service managers and clinical supervisors;
- social workers undergoing qualifying training;
- health service managers undergoing qualifying training;
- those supervising integrated teams;
- newly qualified social workers or those in their first year of practice (ASYE);
- social workers undertaking post-qualifying training;
- practice educators, academic educators and training managers;
- middle managers supervising supervisors;
- senior managers and policy makers.

Recent changes in social work have given an additional responsibility for supervising and assessing newly qualified social workers (NQSWs) within a structured and time limited framework – the Assessed and Supported Year in Employment (ASYE) (SWRB, 2012). Whilst this will give much needed support to the NQSWs, we think supervision will be central to the success of this venture and people charged with this task need to be confident that they have the skills and knowledge necessary to undertake the responsibility.

Crucially we would also suggest that the book is as relevant for supervisees as it is for their supervisors. We have taken a participative approach and in our view both parties can be actively involved in sharing and developing the lessons in this book. In fact the challenge for line managers/supervisors is accepting their role as educators and considering how they might educate and engage their supervisees in a shared endeavour that is essential to the future of our profession and our services.

Current context

A number of high profile reports and inquiries have categorically stated the centrality of supervision to effective social work interventions and professional judgement and decision-making (Laming, 2009; Munro 2011a) and consequently recent reviews of the role of social work have been concerned with making certain that it is fit for purpose.

> *Supervision is an integral element of social work practice, not an add on. Through it social workers review their day to day practice and decision making, plan their learning and development as professionals, and work through the considerable emotional and personal demands the job often places on them*
>
> (Social Work Task Force, 2009)

However, concerns about the frequency and quality of supervision have also been raised. The Social Workers' Workload Survey (Baginsky *et al.*, 2010) reported social workers' criticisms that supervision was reduced to caseload management and targets. Munro's interim report (2011a: 94) concurs and cites evidence indicating the major function of supervision has become managerial oversight to the cost of professional supervision.

> *Reflecting on the sheer scale of the skills and knowledge that are needed to provide effective help for the range of children's needs, the review is led to question the traditional concept of an individual social worker carrying a caseload of many families, receiving only minimal supervision, much of which is overly concerned with management issues than professional casework analysis.*

There have been a number of national initiatives to improve supervision practice. In 2007, the Children's Workforce Development Council and Skills for Care (Skills for Care, 2012a) launched *Providing Effective Supervision*, a workforce development tool designed to provide a model of good practice. Although we have seen little take up, it is a helpful instrument to audit and develop current supervision strategies and practice, and will be referred to in this handbook as providing a useful basis for developing supervision practice.

More recently, and perhaps having a greater impact, the Standards for Employers of Social Workers in England and the Supervision Framework produced by the Social Work Reform Board (SWRB, 2011) have been introduced. These give a clear direction to organisations that supervision needs to be professional and of high quality. The Standards make it clear that it is not sufficient to have a general agreement that supervision takes place; good quality, professional supervision needs to challenge practitioners to reflect critically on their work. All organisations must develop 'a strong culture of supervision, reflective practice and adaptive learning' (SWRB, 2010: 10).

It is worth reproducing the Standards here to be able to consider how they may play a part in improving practice.

Standard 5 of the Standards for Employers of Social Workers in England and the Supervision Framework (SWRB, 2011) states that employers should 'ensure that social workers have regular and appropriate social work supervision' (SWRB, 2011: 8) and lays down explicit benchmarks for agencies to follow:

1. Ensure that social work supervision is not treated as an isolated activity by incorporating it into the organisation's social work accountability framework.

2. Promote continuous learning and knowledge sharing through which social workers are encouraged to draw out learning points by reflecting on their own cases in light of the experiences of peers.

3. Provide regular supervision training for social work supervisors.

4. Assign explicit responsibility for the oversight of appropriate supervision and for issues that arise during supervision.

5. Provide additional professional supervision by a registered social worker for practitioners whose line manager is not a social worker.

6. Ensure that supervision takes place regularly and consistently.

7. Make sure that supervision takes place at least weekly for the first six weeks of employment of a newly qualified social worker, at least fortnightly for the duration of the first six months, and a minimum of monthly supervision thereafter.

8. Ensure that supervision sessions last at least an hour and a half of uninterrupted time.

9. Monitor actual frequency and quality of supervision against clear statements about what is expected.

(SWRB, 2011: 6)

In addition to the Standards, the Reform Board also sets out a framework for supervision. It states that the key elements of effective supervision encompass:

1. quality of decision-making and interventions;

2. line management and organisational accountability;

3. caseload and workload management;

4. identification of further personal learning, career and development opportunities.

(SWRB 2011: 10)

There are two more issues we think are relevant to the current situation:

(a) The Reform Board has issued a clear message that the supervision of adult safeguarding and child protection should be undertaken by a line manager who is a social worker.

(b) The introduction of the Assessed and Supported Year in Employment for NQSWs includes supervision being an integral part of their support.

The overwhelming view is that social work must have effective professional supervision at its core, to ensure professional judgement and critical reflection about decision-making and reasoning as well as the emotional impact. Without this, Munro (2011a) says that social workers will only operate at an intuitive level, risking leaving bias and uncritical thinking unexplored.

Approaches and structure of the book

The difference between this book and others about supervision is that it includes knowledge from perspectives that can offer new insights into developing effective practice. As supervision is a relationship based activity, the ability to form and maintain a professional and productive relationship is at the heart of good practice. In this book we explore the concept of emotional intelligence and how specific interpersonal skills can enhance the relationship. The concept of emotional intelligence is defined by Goleman (1998: 317) as 'the capacity for recognizing our

Table 0.1 Emotional intelligence

	Intrapersonal intelligence/ personal competence	Interpersonal intelligence/ social competence
Awareness	Self-awareness – ability to reflect and accept own feelings	Awareness of others – ability to understand and empathise with the supervisee
Behaviour	Self-management – ability to express and/or contain emotions appropriately	Relationship management – ability to create and maintain relationship with supervisee through all situations

(Adapted from Morrison 2007)

own feelings and those of others, for motivating ourselves, for managing emotions well in ourselves and in our relationships.'

Developing each aspect of emotional intelligence will lead to a greater capacity to manage relationships in supervision. Self-awareness will lead to an understanding and consequently an ability to monitor and manage own emotions. Awareness of own emotions will lead to an appreciation and an understanding of emotions in others. Awareness of the emotions others are experiencing, as well as the ability to manage your own personal emotions, will lead to a greater capacity to manage relationships. Understanding this 'inter-relatedness' is key to being able to work in complex and emotionally charged situations.

There is a growing body of work from psychology and personal development offering a practical set of tools and techniques that can be very useful in supervision. The authors have included models from fields such as neurolinguistic programming, transactional analysis and conflict resolution that offer different strategies on managing self and managing relationships. Using these strategies in the context of supervision can potentially enhance practice.

Another body of knowledge useful for supervisors to develop an understanding about their position and role is leadership theory. Although supervision is often just one of the tasks of the team leader, there is very little written about how the theories, skills and practice from leadership research can inform supervision practice. A number of leadership theories have been included and applied to supervision throughout the book and we believe this adds a depth of analysis that can significantly improve practice.

We have also given the management of supervision and case management careful attention. This is a crucial management function and demands organisational skills and methodical approaches as well as personal effectiveness and leadership skills. Supervision can also not stand alone. It needs to be linked to the broader management of the team and the organisation. Consideration has also been given to how organisations can approach developing supervision and develop a learning culture. This includes the supervision of supervisors.

In seeking to integrate these different dimensions we can be seen to take a 'holistic' approach. There is no 'right' place to start a book that views supervision holistically, because all aspects are inter-related. However we have ordered the book into three themes and sections.

The first section is 'Fundamental concepts' and is probably the most obvious starting point for new supervisors: it includes the essentials of organising and managing supervision and establishing a good practice regime.

The second is called 'Relational aspects' and picks up the theme of emotional intelligence and how to build and maintain a professional and productive supervisory relationship, as well as managing oneself.

The third theme and section locates supervision in its 'Organisational context' and looks at how the quality of supervision can be enhanced by initiatives in the team and workplace.

Good supervision is dependent on the participants being reflective, analytical and critical and so this book includes practice development activities and exercises designed to encourage consideration of aspects of self and practice as well as experimenting with new strategies.

Our overall aim is to develop the *professional understanding, skills and practice* to provide and develop good quality supervision.

Summary: developing capability

This introduction has laid out the foundations of the book. It is clear that, in the current context, supervision is a high profile activity and there are many exhortations to ensure that it needs to be of good quality. However, whilst it is indisputable that high quality supervision is dependent on the ability of the supervisor and the skills and experience they bring to the relationship with their supervisee(s), we also suggest that the organisational context in which supervision takes place can make a significant contribution. The aim to 'facilitate a safe environment for critical reflection, challenge and professional support' (SWRB, 2011: 9) demands considerable cultural change. We believe that the themes developed in this book – ranging across personal effectiveness, the management of supervision, leadership and organisational development – can make a contribution to the development of effective supervisory practice that reaches for the breadth of perspectives necessary for such a complex and demanding endeavour. In candidly engaging supervisors and supervisees, on the grounds that they are the ones best able to develop practice, we hope we have done a little to assist in empowering front-line practitioners and develop both organisational and individual capability.

ACTIVITY O.1

Developing supervisory practice

What changes/initiatives aimed at developing supervisory practice are you experiencing?

Are they offering you ways to develop your personal practice?

What problems would you anticipate and what might you do about them?

Section 1

Fundamental concepts

Chapter 1

Essential principles and first steps

Definitions of supervision

There are many definitions of supervision and an examination of some of them can start the process of developing a personal understanding. It is probably not crucial for everyone to be working to the same definition, but each workplace, agency and supervisory relationship can benefit from establishing principles of good practice.

Here are some to consider:

> A quintessential interpersonal interaction with the general goal that one person, the supervisor, meets with another, the supervisee, in an effort to make the latter more effective in helping people.
>
> (Hess, 1980)

> Professional supervision is a process between someone called a supervisor and another referred to as the supervisee. It is usually aimed at enhancing the helping effectiveness of the person supervised. It may include the acquisition of practice skills, mastery of theoretical or technical knowledge, personal development at the client/therapist interface and professional development.
>
> (Ferguson, 2005, in Davys and Beddoe, 2010)

> Supervision is an accountable process which supports, assures and develops the knowledge, skills and values of an individual, group or team. The purpose is to improve the quality of their work to achieve agreed objectives and outcomes. In social care and children's services this should optimise the capacity of people who use services to lead independent and fulfilling lives.
>
> (SfC/CWDC, 2007)

> Supervision is the primary means by which an agency based supervisor enables staff, individually and collectively; and ensures standards of practice. The aim is to enable supervisees to carry out their work as stated in their job specification as effectively as possible. Regular arranged meetings between supervisors and supervisees form the core of the process by which the supervisory task is carried out. The supervisee is an active participant in this interactional process.
>
> (Brown and Bourne, 1996)

ACTIVITY **1.1**

Definitions of supervision

Consider these definitions of supervision, and use them to create a statement that encapsulates your own view and understanding.

What definition is used by your agency?

How well do the two definitions relate to each other?

Supervisory traditions

There are perhaps two supervisory traditions in the Western organisation of social work, namely, the psychotherapeutic and managerial approaches. We view both as essential to effective social work practice, and so have attempted to bring the best elements of each approach together. Both have their critics, and in more recent times there has been an outcry against managerial policies on the grounds that they depersonalise the service into a target driven economic task (Gould and Baldwin, 2004). However, those of us who can remember the 1970s will also know the concern expressed about a domination of psychotherapeutic social work because of its focus on the individual and not social conditions; psychotherapeutic supervision was seen as over-indulgent and over-focused on the personal development of the supervisee.

There is a tension between the two approaches, yet we would argue that resolving the tensions and developing supervisory practice that embraces both is essential for both supervisors and supervisees, and is perhaps the crucial challenge for supervision. In particular, the exercise of managerial responsibility and power can readily undermine the ethos and processes that are

Table 1.1 Psychotherapeutic and managerial approaches to supervision

Psychotherapeutic approach	Managerial approach
Primary focus is personal growth and development.	Primary focus is case management and service quality.
Often voluntary, supervisees can sometimes choose supervisor. Can be confidential.	Compulsory and supervisor appointed. Not confidential, record kept that is organisational property.
Key processes are reflection and dialogue.	Key process is methodical joint review of cases and their progress.
Focus is on interactions and psychosocial processes.	Focus on needs assessment, objectives, care plans and risk management.
Supervisor usually does not have management responsibility or involvement in workload management.	Supervisor has broader management responsibility including work allocation.
Performance appraisal is usually separated out.	Closely integrated with performance appraisal.

central to the psychotherapeutic approach. The focus on interactions and personal growth means that the psychotherapeutic approach can neglect to address effective case management. Integration of the two approaches, therefore, demands considerable leadership skill, but a richer experience for supervisor and supervisee and better outcomes are the result. Leadership and personal effectiveness, and case management and the management of supervision, therefore, receive equal attention in this handbook.

Functional approaches to supervision

In any book about supervision it is important to acknowledge some of the founding ideas. The early writers conceptualised supervision as fulfilling a number of functions essential to social work practice. Traditionally, three main functions have been portrayed, although as you can see below, different theorists describe them in slightly different terms.

Table 1.2 The functions of supervision – early perspectives

	1	2	3
Kadushin	Educational	Supportive	Administrative
Proctor	Formative	Restorative	Normative
Hawkins	Developmental	Resourcing	Qualitative

(Adapted from Hawkins and Shohet, 2006)

1. Educational/formative/developmental

   This usually refers to the development of the professional skills and knowledge of the supervisee, including understanding the service user and their environment, through reflection on and exploration of the supervisee work. It can also include personal development planning.

2. Supportive/restorative/resourcing

   This involves working with the supervisee to 'unpack' the personal, emotional impact of engaging professionally in highly complex and distressing situations. Hawkins and Shohet (2006) suggest the parallel with the miners needing 'pit head time' to wash off the grime of work rather than take it home.

3. Administrative/normative/qualitative

   This is often seen as the managerial function of supervision, where the supervisor is concerned with standards and quality of work, often because of line management responsibility and accountability. Monitoring of progress in allocated work, performance management and workload within agency policies are integral aspects of this function. Additionally there is also an ethical responsibility that holds the welfare of the users of service as central to any service provision.

Morrison (2005) usefully adds a fourth function of mediation, when the supervisor is an intermediary between the supervisee and other members of staff or parts of the organisation. In this bridging role, the supervisor can be sometimes advocate for workers in the team with senior management or outside agencies and others, promoting organisational policies and developments. This two way process can be challenging for a manager as it can create a tension referred to by Thompson and Gilbert (2011) as 'fighting up and selling down', as it involves balancing (a) supporting the interests of the supervisee with (b) representing the views of the organisation.

Although a functional approach to supervision is often found in organisational policies, and is useful as an overview of expectations, it does, however, have its limitations. For example:

1. It offers a fairly uncritical and static perspective on the role of supervision, and does not consider the complexity of organisations or differences in supervisory relationships.

2. It does not consider the role of power and its manifestations within the supervisory relationship or within the organisation. Power is multifaceted, ever present and socially constructed, and must feature in any analysis.

The dimensions of supervision

We think a more active and dynamic method of exploring supervision is to consider the dimensions of the task. We agree with the argument put forward by Hughes and Pengelly (1997) and Davys and Beddoe (2010) that support is not a function of supervision, but a 'core condition'. This distinction helps supervisors to find the boundary in between a worker's need for support to deliver a good quality service, and their personal development needs. Supervision is an emotionally demanding process involving the use of the personal and, as we mentioned in the previous section, there is a danger of the relationship moving into the 'unchartered territory' of personal therapy. This is not to say that self-understanding and

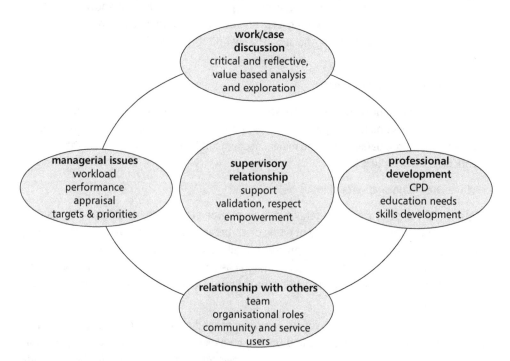

Figure 1.1 The dimensions of supervision

personal development do not happen in supervision, and that any exploration is unwarranted – far from it – they can be a vital ingredient to professional progress. But this model ensures that the supervisor can be clear about the functions of supervision whilst recognising the importance of the relationship on which it is based.

The core dimension is the relationship between supervisor and supervisee and must be grounded in an environment of respect and validation of the individual, which can then lead to a position of empowered support. This acknowledges and works with the role of power in a transparent way. This central dimension influences all the other aspects of supervision.

Work/case discussion is often the main focus of any session but this dimension is more than a cursory glance at the developments since the last meeting; it needs to include the critical reflective analysis demanded by Munro (2011a). It is a skilful exploration of work undertaken that is rich in learning for both parties. The quality of this dimension is often the difference between 'doing' supervision, and the session being a meaningful examination of social work practice.

The managerial dimension is important to include as it will impact on the service generally, as well as individual practice. A robust discussion about targets, performance and workload will have a greater impact than moaning about its presence in supervision. However, it is only one part of the task.

Professional development will cross personal and organisational perspectives. It needs to recognise individual achievements and learning needs but also anticipate future changes in the service and provide developmental opportunities to respond to these.

The final dimension of relating to others recognises that social work is not practised in isolation. A supervisee may have a number of roles and relationships, both in the organisation and externally, that are important in a holistic consideration of practice and personal development.

We hope that it can be seen from Figure 1.1 that all the dimensions are inter-related, and cannot be considered in isolation. Effective supervision involves balancing the system and paying equal attention to all of the dimensions. However, this does not mean a rigid timed agenda for each supervision session. It will be more effective to work towards this being achieved over time, and sometimes a concentrated focus on one dimension may be more productive. What is essential is that as a supervisor, you know when the system is out of balance and take action to bring it back into a dynamic equilibrium.

ACTIVITY *1.2*

Key dimensions of supervision

What for you are the key dimensions of supervision? As the book develops, these dimensions will be explored in more detail, but as a starting point, think about your current supervision practice.

How well do you balance the dimensions of supervision in individual sessions and over a six-month period?

Does it vary between supervisees? What might be causing the variation?

What changes might you put into place to improve the balance?

The management of supervision

The management and organisation of supervision is crucial to ensuring its good quality and meeting the needs of both supervisor and supervisee – so it must be given careful attention. There is a danger in the current climate, where 'managerialist' supervision is criticised, that the importance of the management of supervision and work/case management, which are at the heart of supervision, are sidelined. In our view, as we suggested in the Introduction, both task and relationship matter and need to be integrated. The discussion below focuses on your responsibilities as a supervisor, but it is worth bearing in mind that supervisees also have some responsibility for the effective management of supervision so that it is not something that is done to them. Rather it should be approached as a shared activity that sets a foundation for the quality of the experience for both supervisor and supervisee.

Contracts, agreements and the beginnings of supervision

There is an established history of contracts being seen as important to supervisory practice, recognising that these define boundaries and provide a structure for the relationship, and many organisations now have pro forma written contracts. There is a danger that these can be rather superficial in that they only cover the practicalities such as timing, frequency, length, location, recording, agenda setting and arrangements for cancellation. These issues are important, but they do nothing to really mould the quality of the future supervisory relationship. A contract that looks only at practicalities may create a rather sterile supervision and meaningless evaluation which merely ensures that supervision 'happened', irrespective of its quality. This sort of contract is often never referred to again.

One of the purposes of a meaningful contract is to give the supervisee a say in their supervision and to lay a shared foundation. Presenting them with a bureaucratic fait accompli over which they have no control is a bad start. Another purpose of a contract is to shape behaviour to provide a quality relationship that can consider all the dimensions of the supervisory tasks and deliver the agreed outcomes. The aim is to develop an environment of trust, respect and openness (as in the core of Figure 1.1 on page 6). The contract can also provide the basis for evaluating supervision and is therefore the key to improving supervision. This 'deeper' level of contracting is sometimes referred to as the 'psychological contract' (Carroll and Gilbert, 2005) and is crucial in co-creating a safe and facilitative environment.

However, developing this type of contract, which goes beyond the practicalities, is actually quite hard and many supervisors struggle with how to approach it. We suggest the following guidelines for good contracting.

Guidelines for good contracting

Prepare – you are centre stage in this and the impression you give can set the foundation for the rest of the relationship, so plan for it carefully and allow plenty of time. We know how pressured you are, but you won't get a worthwhile contract that can support quality supervision if you try to deal with it in a few minutes; rather, you will end up with a shallow list of practicalities. See it as an opportunity to 'set out your stall' as a supervisor and leader, engage the supervisee in your philosophy and approach, and find out their views.

You may need to spread contracting over two sessions with chance for some thinking in between. So perhaps set up some of the issues identified below for discussion at the next meeting and ask the supervisee to think about them between times.

Trust – remember there may be ambivalence at the beginning of a new supervisory relationship, even if you have a pre-existing good relationship. Both parties may need to take risks and acknowledge fears and apprehension about the new relationship, disclosing hitherto unknown information. You may need to take the lead in this and provide reassurance about allowing supervision to be a safe place for the supervisee to work with the emotional and stressful aspects of the role. A discussion about openness and boundaries is also important in establishing trust with each other.

Rights and responsibilities – this can be a difficult discussion, but talking about the supervisee's previous experiences can be quite a good opening. Ask the supervisee about what has worked or not worked for them or what has made supervision rewarding or unrewarding. Now might be the time to flag up the importance of reflective practice, emotional support, giving feedback and working together to improve professional practice. You can also ask them what they do well as a supervisee and what they would like to improve on. Contribute your views on what makes for good quality supervision and share what you think your strengths and weaknesses as a supervisor are. Then agree 'ground rules' together that will support the positives you have identified together and avoid the negatives.

Control and power – these are often the areas that are sidestepped, but are always at the centre of relationships. Being open to the supervisee's views and being clear about your perceptions will start to address these issues (see next chapter for further discussion).

Personal development – emphasise the importance of personal development. Ask them what their previous experiences of planning for their personal development have been, what has been most effective in improving their practice and what has been less beneficial. Identify any particular learning styles or needs they might have and build objectives for developing their practice into the contract; invite them also to raise with you any other matters relating to their wellbeing, such as what they are enjoying in their work and what might be getting in their way. Discuss how you will approach learning from supervision and outline how you will manage training together (see Chapter 6).

Appraisal and assessments – address these issues from the beginning. Discuss each other's expectations and previous experiences. Discuss and agree how to give feedback; some may need this frequently at the beginning as a way of building their confidence, whilst constant detailed feedback can be an irritant to others. Ask them about their career hopes and aspirations, and what may help them achieve their objectives and ensure they are enjoying their work. Discuss how you might both make the formal processes meaningful. Agree how performance issues will be managed and encourage them to identify these themselves, in order to gain support and possibly raise organisational problems that are affecting their practice. ASYE assessments, probationary periods and reviews will cause anxiety for the supervisee, and transparency about the process and your role in their assessment is crucial for a good working relationship.

Deal with the practicalities – only at the end look at the practicalities, but focus on those that are crucial to the quality of supervision, such as how you will both prepare and avoid and how you will manage interruptions and cancellations. Also give some thought to meeting your supervisees' needs. Once a month for an hour and a half might be the 'bottom line' frequency and length, but can they ask for earlier or extra sessions? Can newer and less experienced team members receive more? Key dimensions are:

- preparing for supervision, avoiding interruptions, location, creating a comfortable environment, confidentiality;

- scheduling, length, frequency, cancellations and rescheduling;

- setting agendas, recording and agreeing content and decisions/disagreements;

- debrief/feedback at the end of a supervision session and planning for the next.

Build in review and evaluation – finally, review the content of the contract and check out that your supervisee agrees with it and ask if they have been happy with the process of formulating it. Agree how and when you will evaluate supervision and your joint contract together. Make sure this actually happens – perhaps building it into your appraisal session. Contracting is key to the management of supervision and you will know if you have made it meaningful when it becomes a point of reference rather than being consigned to a file.

REFLECTION POINT

Reflect on your own practice for negotiating and agreeing contracts.

What do you do well? What aspects could be improved – and how will you carry this out?

Case and practice management and structuring supervision

As a social work supervisor, you have usually been given direct responsibility for managing a colleague's work. Your authority to supervise is usually supported by other functions and powers such as the power to appoint, the power to promote, reward and regrade, the power to discipline, suspend or dismiss.

The primary purpose of supervision is to allow you to manage the quality of your supervisee's work or, if you like, their performance. You have been appointed to do this on behalf of the organisation on the basis of your experience and expertise. You also have responsibility for their professional development, their personal support and their health and safety.

Supervisees also have responsibility for their own practice, their continuing professional development (CPD) and their health and safety, but ultimately, however, responsibility rests with you and you are accountable for their work as well as their welfare. Only rarely will you have to impose decisions, confront a performance problem or begin capability procedures, but if you identify quality problems in supervision, you will need to intervene.

This means case or practice management should be at the heart of supervision – it is what supervision is for. Handled well, the process of managing practice in supervision is, however, also the most effective method for developing practice and supporting a team member.

Case and performance management aren't therefore optional: you are quite simply responsible and accountable for your team's work. The current debate, that suggests supervision will be improved by a developmental approach rather than one that is focused only on case and performance management, doesn't mean an either/or approach, but that the two should be integrated to achieve best practice. This is made clear by the Social Work Reform Board's agenda for supervision.

Supervision should:

- improve the quality of decision-making and interventions;

- enable effective line management and organisational accountability;

- identify and address issues related to caseloads and workload management;

- help to identify and achieve personal learning, career and development opportunities.

(SWRB, 2011)

Your effectiveness in managing practice will depend on your approach: it's not what you do, it's the way that you do it. Your personal skills and leadership are necessary to ensure that it is an empowering and enabling process rather than purely controlling and disempowering.

The case management process

Case or practice management is a problem-solving process which provides a methodical way of approaching any difficulty and bringing planned improvement. It also provides a systematic process to reflect on practice.

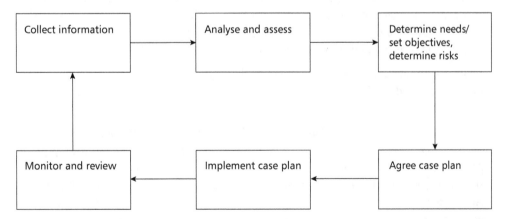

Figure 1.2 The case management process

Typically, cases allocated to a social worker are reviewed and discussed in supervision and this process shapes the discussion. For instance, in a newly allocated case, it is important initially that the right information is being collected, then it is important that this is analysed to determine needs or set objectives, and that these are then used to develop a case plan. Later supervision sessions then monitor implementation and review progress. Sometimes plans break down, situations change or new information becomes available which means that the analysis and assessment, needs or objectives and care plan all need to be changed. Sometimes it is clear that the plan has been successfully implemented and the case can be closed.

The case management process might appear to be simple, but it is very important that it is used reflectively and not just followed superficially. When there are problems it can be helpful to refer to Figure 1.3 to help to identify where the difficulties stem from.

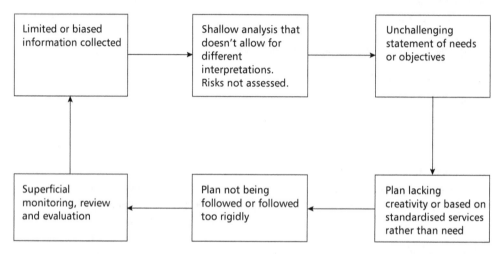

Figure 1.3 A problematic case management process

Each supervisee may need a different approach when using this process. For example, an experienced social worker will usually present cases to you in supervision guided by the principles of case management as a problem-solving process. They will identify issues that need consideration and perhaps decisions that need to be made and they may also suggest what should now be done or identify some options, often offering their evaluation of them. They may also identify anything they are finding difficult or are unsure of.

A less experienced supervisee or practitioner with a complex case may need to be prompted with questions and not be able to propose a way forward. They may need support to follow the process.

Better supervisory practice gives depth to each of the stages of the case management process through critical reflection and, in essence, the stance you take is that you help them problem solve and case manage, developing their expertise to do this so that they become increasingly independent as a practitioner. Supervision offers them chance to reflect on their progress, share concerns and their analysis, and reflect on their practice. Using the model of situational leadership (see page 35) will help you to gauge the right level of intervention.

There is a danger that case management can become too regimented and based on a mechanical review of each case. Limited time can also lead to shortcutting, jumping to actions without proper analysis. Effective supervision demands hard and soft skills. The hard skills are method and structure based on the case management process, but these are not enough; they have to be combined with the 'soft' skills needed to develop reflection and independent practice.

The joy of being a supervisor is the challenge that comes from needing to combine method and structure with empowerment and reflection. You are assisting your supervisees to develop their practice and become increasingly independent as professionals and you also get to share their practice with them. In fact, it is a huge privilege to be allowed such an intimate view of their experiences and their thinking and share in their growth and development, as well as working together to enhance service quality and service outcomes.

REFLECTION POINT

How effective is your case management? Do cases have clearly identified needs/objectives and plans? Are these reviewed regularly and adjusted?

Can you see your supervisees preparing more effectively and taking increased responsibility for their practice?

Structuring and planning supervision

Supervision needs to be structured and planned, and the dimensions diagram (Figure 1.1) can be a good template on which to base an agenda. As work/case management can dominate or even overwhelm the time for supervision, it is important to plan for parts of sessions or some whole sessions to be devoted to the other dimensions (as indicated in the Introduction). That is not to say that work/case management does not involve professional and personal develop-ment; it does. It is only to suggest that dedicated sessions allow opportunity to reflect on and explore the less urgent but equally as important issues, and reflect on topics that may have arisen as a theme in different sessions. This means careful scheduling of planned supervision sessions and we suggest whole sessions are occasionally set aside for wider professional reflection and review.

Determining the agenda for a session and preparing for supervision

In addition to long-term scheduling, planning and preparing for each session is crucial and will have a big impact on the quality of supervision. Preparation time is important for both of you, so schedule this into your diary before a session, ensuring there are gaps between sessions if you are supervising several people. We know it isn't easy given the pressures you are under, but it is essential. At the very least, you need to remind yourself of actions from the last session so these can be reviewed, but briefing yourself on the supervisee's work and cases by reviewing the records can be really helpful and might mean you spot something that has been missed or could be approached differently. It is also crucial to remember that the supervision is about the supervisee and not just the work; allow some time to reflect on how supervision with that particular person is progressing in relation to the contract and what you might be trying to achieve in the session.

Agreeing an outline agenda with your supervisee in advance will aid preparation. However, it is always wise to check this again at the start of a session to accommodate a crisis or new priority that has arisen. Having a standardised agenda can be unhelpful, although some organisations have adopted this approach. Determining priorities and shaping an individual session in the context of the whole that constitutes the supervisory relationship is one of a supervisor's skills.

Every piece of work or case cannot be discussed in each session, so prioritising, as well as overall monitoring and reviewing of workload, is essential. It may also not be necessary to have a slot for professional and personal development in each session. Rather it is important that all dimensions receive sufficient attention over time. Reflecting on the session should be a feature of each meeting, and will help to ensure supervision is responding to the needs of all parties.

Recording

It is crucial that a record is kept of supervision and that discussions and decisions are also added to the case record. Usually the supervisor takes responsibility for this and often the record of supervision is signed off by supervisor and supervisee.

Recording is problematic not in the least because it is very time consuming. You will need to be concise, but, as well as decisions, you will need to try to capture the essence of what was discussed. Supervisors sometimes record sessions on a PC or laptop as the supervision session progresses, but this means they are not giving full attention to their supervisee, and keeping a record may easily take over the task of listening and encouraging critical reflection. Supervisees have been known to complain that a supervisor typing and staring at the screen is a huge distraction; for a supervisor, looking up to find your supervisee quietly sobbing can be rather a sobering event.

Pausing to record at intervals may be an option, or it may simply be necessary to keep written notes that are less intrusive during a session, then record afterwards. Reviewing and agreeing the record at the start of the next session can be too late; decisions get lost and differences in opinion may not be identified in time. Also, if you get distracted and it is some time before you make the record, even with notes, remembering complex discussions can be hard. So you may need to build in recording time at the end of a session. There is also the option of reviewing your notes at a natural break in the session, such as at the end of a particular case discussion. This can offer a useful summary, before moving on.

Whatever approach you adopt, you need to meet several objectives:

- a concise, accurate and timely record of main discussions and decisions made;
- agreement of the record;
- a copy included in relevant case files or records;
- a process that does not disrupt your interaction with your supervisee;
- a process that is mutually agreed with the supervisee.

Cancellation and rescheduling

Cancellation of supervision sessions because of crises is often common and it can seriously undermine the quality of supervisory practice. Cancelling a session even for good reasons can undermine the timely review of cases and there can be a domino effect, with sessions constantly being cancelled and rescheduled taking up vast amounts of time and energy, with little actual supervision happening.

It is important that you establish the principle that supervision should only be cancelled in the case of dire emergencies or illness and establish a procedure for doing so. A session should be immediately rescheduled as near as the cancelled time as possible. Leave some gaps in your diary to try to accommodate what should be rare cancellations, and expect supervisees if necessary to move things around to accommodate this. It is an area where establishing a clear line can pay; if a team culture develops where cancellation is easy, you can not only end up with a scheduling nightmare but also lose oversight of cases and their management. As the leader of the team, your demonstration of good practice will draw others to follow you.

REFLECTION POINT

Do you have an effective process for scheduling sessions in the long term and setting session agendas that ensures a balance of areas addressed?

Are accurate and concise records of sessions made promptly and in such a way as not to impose on the discussion? Are key issues and discussions in supervision also added to the case record? Are records agreed?

Do you have clear and effective procedures for cancellation and rescheduling?

Have you developed a team culture and processes that give priority to supervision?

Chapter 2
Strategies in supervision

Most of this text is concerned with formal, planned and usually one-to-one supervision sessions, but it is important to recognise that there are different types of supervision that can also play an important role in supporting professional practice and practice development. What is usually referred to as 'informal supervision' has two main types.

One is an unplanned discussion and exploration of a case with you or other members of the team. This is an important process as it allows a social worker to explore their analysis of a situation and possible options and responses and can be an important way of developing a care plan. However, it shouldn't be seen as a substitute for formal planned supervision as the place to discuss cases and agree decisions.

The second type of informal supervision is better termed 'consultation'. Consultation occurs when a development in a case means that a social worker needs to consult urgently with you outside of the normal planned supervision sessions. A consultation can be and often is a decision-making point, and decisions and the circumstances that have generated them need to be recorded.

Group supervision

Group and/or peer supervision is becoming more popular, usually as an additional feature of supervisory support and sometimes, but rarely, as the sole method. There are advantages and disadvantages as outlined in Table 2.1.

Group supervision is most effective in situations where there are a limited number of cases and the group needs to work as a team. So, for instance, a multi-disciplinary ward meeting in a hospital allows the team to review the case of each resident, working together in analysing need, reviewing progress and agreeing care plans and actions. Residential and day care can benefit from a similar process and there is an interesting question as to whether the user/resident should be present (see section on communities of practice on page 99).

Group supervision is easier to manage if it is focused on practice development, for both the individual and the group. Individual supervision can occur alongside, offering individual attention and picking up on the other core dimensions. Used in this way, group members can present a case they need help with, or one that will be useful to share with the group as an exemplar. As the management of the case will be dealt with in individual supervision, many of the possible disadvantages can be avoided.

Table 2.1 Advantages and disadvantages of group supervision

Advantages	Disadvantages
1. Supportive environment. 2. Input from other colleagues, not just supervisor, can provide a wider range of perspectives and allow for the sharing of expertise. 3. Saving time, although the planning needed may make this less than initially thought. 4. Learning from one another. 5. Case plans are agreed across the team allowing collaboration; team has knowledge of one anothers' work.	1. Less time available for each supervisee and 'keeping things safe' can make discussion superficial. 2. Group dynamics can be very powerful and difficult to manage and so become the focus of attention. 3. Presenting the case to a group can be challenging; the supervisee can find themselves put 'on the spot' and sharing sensitive material can be difficult for them. 4. Supervisor/manager can be sidelined and forced to watch the group condoning or proposing poor practice or ignoring good. 5. Recording and keeping track of cases can be difficult.

Whatever the reasons for conducting group supervision, Hawkins and Shohet (2006) urge that it must come from positive choice, rather than compromise or enforcement. Success will be dependent on the members valuing the gains from the group and not feeling it is second best. Munro has suggested that the case review process she developed (which the government has now made the basis for serious case reviews) be extended to review other cases, including those that are going well so that a team and an organisation can develop the quality of services (SCIE, 2012a). This could make a good basis for a group supervision session and it is worth taking a look at the Social Care Institute of Excellence (SCIE) resources and referring to Williams *et al.* (2012), another book in this series, which focuses on promoting organisational learning.

Managing and leading group supervision

Contracting

As with individual supervision, the contracting and ground rules are imperative and in some ways need to be even more carefully considered because there are multiple differences between members. A group that only comes together for supervision will have a very different dynamic from one that is already a team for other purposes and has an inter-related life outside of supervision. For example, a supervision group in a residential unit where everyone knows all the users will be different to a team of social workers who work independently. Experience, status, hidden agendas and personal/professional relationships may all play a part in the coherence of the group, and so the intention and boundaries for the group need to be clear and agreed. Some questions to consider are:

- What is the size and membership of the group and what determines its boundaries?

- What is the reason for the group being set up?

- Is it open or closed, compulsory or optional?

- What is to be discussed and how will the agenda be set?

- What is agreed about confidentiality and recording?

- How often, when and where are the meetings?

- Can it make decisions or only make proposals?

Facilitation or leadership of the group

This needs to be part of the initial contract and agreement. Many of the problems in groups can arise from woolly discussions about who and how a group is facilitated. Using Proctor's model (2000), four types of groups and leadership styles can be distinguished.

1. Authoritative: the leader/supervisor conducts 1:1 supervision with other members watching.

2. Participative: the leader is responsible for the conduct and direction of the meeting. Participants are invited to contribute by the leader.

3. Cooperative: where there is a facilitator who holds the group boundaries and leaves supervision to the group members. Within this style there are various options; for example, will the facilitator take responsibility for timings, agenda keeping, summarising and focusing the discussion and acknowledging difficulties?

4. Peer group: where all group members take joint responsibility for everything. A clear structure is important to ensure the group stays within boundaries and keeps to the aims of the group.

No one style is necessarily better than another and will be dependent on the aims of the group. Your style may evolve as the group develops, but any change needs to be combined with transparency and agreement. For example, setting up a cooperative group and then taking over the supervision, because you want certain issues raised, is unlikely to work.

Setting ground rules to assist with shaping behaviour can be a helpful way forward. This can be based on individual group members sharing what they have found most useful and unhelpful in sharing their practice with groups. As well as establishing guidance that will influence how individuals conduct themselves, this also, through sharing, builds trust and respect.

Structuring the session

The content of a group session and how it is structured needs to be agreed and clear to all participants. It can range from timed supervision sessions for all participants to one person bringing a case scheduled in advance. Creative use of role play, sculpts and other techniques can provide alternative insights to a case discussion.

The session can also include other activities, such as a 'what's on top' session at the beginning, to identify and deal with priorities, with informal time at the end where less urgent issues can be dealt with. However, clear boundaries are important to prevent drift or avoidance of difficult issues.

Group dynamics

Group behaviours can be powerful and knowledge of group work theories and group process are important for a facilitator/supervisor and group members. However, for a group to progress successfully, the facilitator and/or the group members also need the understanding and confidence to challenge behaviours as the group develops. For example, some group stage theories (e.g. Tuckman, 1965) will suggest there is a conflict stage where tensions and differences need to be worked through – this is often called 'storming' and a common feature can be conflict with the group leader. The group will require careful guidance through this phase to be able to work effectively and you might need personal support. A new group may not work well at first and may need direction and leadership before becoming more productive and less dependent as it develops.

Responsibility for acknowledging and managing the dynamics generated by a group is important. This is an important role for the group leader to manage, as it has the capacity to make or break a group. So, for instance, a group giving positive feedback following a case discussion can be very rewarding and motivating, but negative or critical comments at an early stage in the group can be received as personal censure and be very stressful. Practice can only be effectively challenged when sufficient trust and respect have been developed, and then it can be more effective than anything an individual supervisor can provide.

There are advantages and disadvantages to all methods, and careful thought should be given to the setting up of the group to maximise the positives and minimise the negatives. Groups, at their best, are a powerful and creative resource for all members. It can also be a challenging role for a supervisor, especially as a storming group is likely to challenge you and your power. So, ongoing personal supervision, as well as initial training, is vital – particularly for someone undertaking group supervision for the first time.

REFLECTION POINT

Can you see advantages to introducing group supervision as part of your supervisory practice? If you are already using it, what do you see as its benefits?

Should you choose to introduce it, what problems might you anticipate or what problems have you already experienced?

What steps might you take to ensure you introduce group supervision effectively, or what steps might you take to improve group supervision?

How do you/will you get support to analyse and debrief from leading a group supervision session?

Supervision strategies

There is a tendency to assume that there is only one type of supervision and one way to practice, whereas in fact there are many different settings which demand different approaches or strategies. For instance, we can identify six different scenarios that require different approaches and combinations of methods (see Table 2.2).

Table 2.2 Supervision strategies

Setting	Challenges	Typical structure
Fieldwork team based in the same location supervised by their manager.	Probably the most common scenario that this book and others tend to talk to and policy tends to address.	As described in this book, focused on regular planned supervision sessions supported by informal and group supervision.
Fieldwork team with a supervisory team.	All the issues raised in this book with the addition of potentially several supervisors being involved in formal and informal supervision.	Focus on regular managed formal supervision supported by informal consultation; leadership and supervision of the supervisory team is necessary to ensure consistency and avoid confusion over decisions.
Dispersed team – e.g. emergency duty team.	Limited face-to-face and team contact, reliance on technology to communicate, incident management rather than case management.	More informal contact demanding high order communication skills from the supervisor to overcome limitations of IT. Less frequent formal supervision sessions and team working opportunities.
Reception and assessment team.	Cases closed before formal supervision happens. Supervisor has to supervise 'on the hoof'. Recording decisions from consultations as they go. Reflection can be a challenge.	Dominated by informal supervision/consultation, with formal supervision offering opportunity to reflect.
Residential or day care team	Everyday contact and working together delivering the service as the team gives supervisors direct knowledge of practice but wider team is in effect drawn into supervision.	Informal supervision, group supervision and team working dominate with reduced formal supervision. Community of practice approach, user participation and involvement are easier.

Table 2.2 Continued

Setting	Challenges	Typical structure
Integrated multi-professional team	Professional and management supervision can be separated out with resulting problems of responsibilities and communication. Danger of one dominating or getting lost.	Twin track provision that demands policy and practices to manage the interface.

ACTIVITY 2.1

Supervision strategies

Which of the above settings is similar to your own?

Which approaches are you using?

How well does the 'mix' or strategy work? What challenges does it present you with?

Mediation

The Effective Supervision Unit (SfC/CWDC, 2007) suggests that there is a need for a supervisor to 'identify wider issues and raise them appropriately in the organisation and with other stakeholders'. Some writers (Morrison, 2005) have suggested that this activity – 'mediation' – is a function of supervision.

The power of individual supervision is that it links an individual's practice to the wider network that supports it. The process is two way: issues identified by the individual as they practice are fed into the network and issues arising in the network are fed into supervision. For instance, it can identify quality problems which the wider organisation needs to act on, and new organisational policy can be communicated and carried directly into practice. It is thus both a rich source of information and a key point where information can be disseminated. Mediation by a supervisor realises and releases this power. The essence of mediation is communication, and supervision could be seen as the centre of a communication hub. Sometimes, though, it can involve more than communication in that you may need to persuade and negotiate in order for part of the network to take action and engage with you.

At best you will find the network responsive. So, for instance, your manager might be proactive in encouraging you to raise issues you identify in supervision with them, so they can raise them with senior managers. Other departments or co-providers might be keen to work with you on common problems or issues. On other occasions you will have to open up communication and negotiate for changes to happen. There are also systems that can help; for instance, a business planning system in an organisation allows you to identify with the team organisational issues that need a response, and develop strategies to respond to issues identified by the team as needing attention. Training audits can help you respond to development needs you identify in

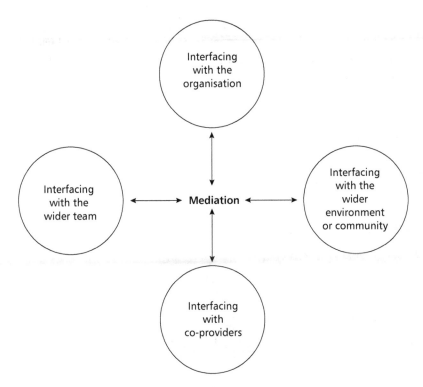

Figure 2.1 Key dimensions of mediation

supervision, and joint planning arrangements can help you work with co-providers on service improvements.

Interfacing with the wider team

Your team activity is perhaps as important as your supervisory activity, both supporting it and being supported by it. There are some very useful team activities that can be used to help develop the team:

- taking common quality problems identified in supervision and problem solving and negotiating a shared improvement plan;

- identifying a common unmet user need and putting together a project or policy proposal;

- reviewing the quality of supervision together and devising a team supervision improvement plan;

- sharing, as case studies in group supervision, cases identified in supervision that would benefit from group problem solving or that should be shared as examples of good practice;

- using team expertise, and perhaps drawing on outside help, to put together a team learning event to respond to a shared need identified in supervision;

- identifying common communication breakdowns or misunderstandings in supervision and clarifying them in a team meeting.

Really, you need regular team meetings and a team development agenda to run alongside supervision. This is beautifully illustrated by Adair's action-centred leadership model (Figure 2.2) where working both with the team and with individuals in supervision supports the team's shared task of delivering the service.

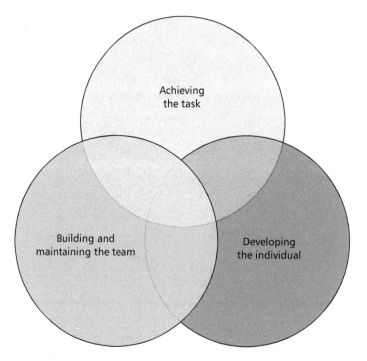

Figure 2.2 Adair's action-centred leadership model (Adair, 1983: 44)

Interfacing with the organisation

It needs to be recognised that, particularly in relation to the wider organisation, mediation has in part a controlling function. For instance, a supervisor on behalf of the organisation has responsibility for ensuring that an employee is clear about their responsibilities and the organisational procedures they must follow. They also have the responsibility to intervene on behalf of the organisation if there are performance or contractual problems. This is balanced by a supervisor having responsibility for ensuring that an organisation's duty of care is met in protecting an employee's physical and emotional health and wellbeing. There is currently a welcome interest in improving workplace wellbeing and you should visit the wellbeing website on **www.dwp.gov.uk/health-work-and-well-being/**.

Table 2.3 gives an indication of the information that can be taken into supervision and the information you may need to take out of supervision to the organisation.

Table 2.3 Information taken into/out of supervision

Information in	Information out
Organisational responsibilities, procedures and standards	Performance and contractual problems
Organisational plans and strategy	Quality problems and problems with meeting service standards (including those for provision of supervision)
New policy, procedures or systems	Proposed changes/improvements in policy, systems and procedures and services arising from supervision
Budgets	Spending
Organisational performance information	Performance information
Available training opportunities	Training needs
Vacancies	Workload and resourcing issues

Interfacing with the wider environment or community

Table 2.4 considers what information might be exchanged with the wider community. Furthermore, a supervisor also has responsibility for ensuring professional codes of practice are adhered to, and needs to mediate on behalf of professional bodies (the Health and Care Professions Council became the regulatory body for Social Work from 1 August 2012). The SWRB has published standards for employers that are ready for implementation. These emphasise the importance of supervision and the role of the supervisor in supporting and protecting their staff (see Introduction for current context).

Being proactive in involving people who use services, and carers, in reviewing and developing services is an important dimension of interfacing with the wider community. It can be seen as a way of anchoring the service to ensure that it meets needs and provides outcomes for service users.

Table 2.4 Exchange of information with the wider community

Information in	Information out
Customer feedback on services	Information about services and resources
New needs or needs not being met	Proposals for new services or developing services
Their views on proposed service developments	Responses to their views
Changes in the community that can affect services	Changes in policy and practice, local and national

Interfacing with co-providers

Table 2.5 Areas of information that may need mediation with co-providers

Information in	Information out
New needs they identify or service improvement proposals	New needs you identify or service improvement proposals
Quality problems they identify	Quality problems you identify
Changes in their policy and practice	Changes in your policy and practice
Individual care plans and information about cases	Individual care plans and information about cases

Team members will be in independent contact with professionals from other organisations and in forums where they will interact with other organisational managers. They will also perhaps have contact with community groups that you don't. Mediation is therefore perhaps best seen as a joint responsibility, with both supervisor and supervisee playing a part in managing this wider process of service delivery. Sometimes you will be able to more readily pick up an issue yourself and move it on, but sometimes you will find that a joint approach is more useful. For instance, members of the team might even be delegated responsibility for liaising with co-providers on behalf of the team.

Some of the supervisors we have worked with describe the experience of mediating as being caught between competing demands and needs, and feeling as if you are 'stuck between a rock and a hard place'. There is no doubt mediation can be a demanding dimension of supervisory practice; however, it is also an important opportunity to influence and bring positive change. It therefore demands considerable leadership and also awareness of the role of power in our organisations and in service delivery. We have made managing power the basis of the next chapter.

ACTIVITY 2.2

Mediation and action-centred leadership

Review the dimensions outlined above. What are the strengths and weaknesses of your mediation? What could you work on?

Is your leadership 'action-centred' – combining and balancing supervision with developing the team and achieving the task?

Assessment role for supervisors

With the introduction of the Assessed and Supported Year in Employment (ASYE), there is now an increasing expectation that supervisors will take on formal assessment of social work practice as a specific responsibility for newly qualified social workers. As supervisors you have always had an assessment task and this is obvious within the appraisal and performance management dimensions. However, there seems to be an increased nervousness about assessment in the context of making a decision about newly qualified workers passing or failing their ASYE, so it is worth spending some time understanding the new framework, as well as considering how you will undertake the assessment.

The Professional Capabilities Framework (PCF) will provide the assessment structure and is the new comprehensive framework for professional development across all areas of social work practice, developed by the SWRB. It comprises nine domains, within which is a subset of capability statements specific to the career level. Assessment using the PCF is to be 'holistic' and designed to move away from a competence-based process to one which is based on overall capability. For you as a supervisor this will mean that your assessment will consider their practice against the PCF as a whole; recognising the inter-relatedness of the nine capability domains and the complexity of social work practice. Practitioners will need to demonstrate integration of their knowledge and skills and be able to generalise their learning to other aspects of their work. Your assessment will therefore be, first, an overall judgement of quality of performance, and then be a more detailed report using the capability statements. The individual capability statements will be important in providing the detail of how the expectations for the capabilities have been met, as well as identifying gaps or areas of concern.

The assessment of the ASYE is envisaged to be progressive over the year, leading to an effective summative judgement. Most ASYE schemes will have a set of expectations for supervisors and supervisees. This will usually comprise learning agreements and reviews, supervision requirements, observation and other assessment requirements. As it is a set period of time, it will be important to keep on top of the time scales.

There are a number of different stages to the process of assessment (Walker *et al.*, 2008, and Williams and Rutter, 2010) which, for our purposes, can be summarised as follows:

1. Planning. The learning agreement will be a key place for planning the year, and you will need to be proactive in ensuring that there are sufficient and varied opportunities for the newly qualified social worker to meet their learning needs as well as demonstrate their capability. The ASYE is not only about assessment, but also meeting the worker's learning needs. This is discussed much more in the rest of the book, but is important to remember here, so that the balance of your role is maintained. The strength of the ASYE scheme is that it is a progressive assessment, and so regular feedback and reviews to assess the *development* of practice over the year is crucial to maintaining a holistic perspective.

   - What is assessed? The basis of the ASYE is that newly qualified social workers will be assessed holistically using the PCF. So take some time to get to grips with this new capability framework. Consider which of the domains interact together and where issues may overlap and be relevant to more than one capability.

   - How will you assess? The ASYE scheme will require a portfolio of evidence to be produced by the NQSW to demonstrate their professional capability. You may be required to observe practice in different environments and at different times during the year. But the essence of achieving a positive experience is how you work with your supervisee to match the learning objectives with the observation and evidence requirements. What opportunities do you think will provide a good learning experience for your supervisee?

2. Making judgements. What is good enough practice is a question that does not have a definitive answer. When planning a learning/assessment opportunity, it can be helpful to have a discussion with your supervisee to tease out what the expectations are. Perhaps consider having three criteria (poor, good enough, good) for judging an observation and have a couple of agreed statements that describe the practice for each. This can then help to structure feedback.

3. Collecting the evidence. The ASYE scheme and final report template will probably outline what the newly qualified worker needs to provide as evidence. However, you can also be proactive in gaining feedback from other professionals throughout the year. Supervision notes are likely to be a rich source of evidence for your summative report, as well as observations of practice and critical reflections. As the ASYE is seen as a progressive assessment, evidence of development of capability will be helpful as you work towards your summative decision of whether the worker has passed the year.

4. Weighing the evidence; making a final judgement. The task of making a final decision is complex and will contain elements of subjectivity. Although you have the PCF as a measure, you still have the responsibility of deciding what is an acceptable standard of practice in your context. Some questions that might help you to make a decision are:

   • Is it relevant? Is there a clear relationship between the evidence and the capability? Does it relate to the capability being assessed completely, partially or not at all?

   • Is it valid? Does the piece of practice provide suitable evidence for this assessment in this context?

   • Is it sufficient? Does the evidence presented demonstrate capability to the depth and proficiency you would expect at this level?

   • Is it reliable? Is there evidence across a varied range of situations for you to be convinced that the worker has a universal capability? An additional method of judging whether your evidence is good enough is to use the concept of triangulation (Williams and Rutter, 2010). Triangulation is when you have a number of pieces of evidence from different sources that prove the same capability. For example, you may demonstrate that you 'recognise and manage the impact on people of the power invested in your role' (capability statement 3.3) in a reflective analysis of an assessment as well as in a direct observation write-up. This triangulation increases the strength of evidence and many schemes may ask the worker to provide more than one piece of evidence in the portfolio.

5. Is it agreed? As we have stressed throughout this book, it is important to be working in partnership with your supervisee, and this is no exception. Regular feedback and reviews will be a feature of the ASYE scheme, as is critical reflection and evaluation. All the way through the year, the supervisee should have a good idea of the progress being made, and areas of development that are needed and areas of concern. Your judgement will therefore need to be evidence based, and delivered with an understanding that they may have a different perspective (see section on giving feedback for further discussion, page 81).

6. Documenting your decision. It is likely that you will have a template to complete, and again it is likely that you will be asked firstly to make a holistic assessment about their professional

practice before a longer more detailed report that provides an evaluation of their practice against the nine domains. Take time to write the report; it is an important document for both you and your supervisee. It will be part of their CPD portfolio for many years and deserves to be constructed thoughtfully. Make sure you block out space to give good attention to its completion.

ACTIVITY **2.3**

Preparing for assessment

Think through your role in any assessment situation.

*Use the six points above to write down how **you** will undertake the assessment and what you need to do to make that a positive learning experience for your supervisee.*

*For further information about the PCF and ASYE, please go to The College of Social Work website, as there are new materials and statements being posted regularly: **www.collegeof socialwork.org/home/**.*

Chapter 3
Power and leadership in supervision

As we have outlined in the Introduction, there has been much recent debate and concern about supervision having changed in the last two decades from having a holistic focus on professional practice to only being concerned with managerial issues of work output and evaluation, that is, performance management (Noble and Irwin, 2009; Munro, 2011a). These critics argue that supervision was once developmental and one of the few places where critical reflection and analysis, using research and theory, could result in informed and evidence-based practice. The dominance of a managerial perspective, they argue, has resulted in a target driven monitoring of activity, with supervision dominated by administrative and organisational issues. Cuts in services and overworked front-line teams experiencing supervision on the run can only increase the possibility of supervision being superficial and too managerial.

However, it must also be recognised that the dominance of professionalism and professional development can also be unhelpful. For instance, it could be suggested that in the past supervision has sometimes been too focused on a social worker's personal development, which is why the Health and Care Professions Council deliberately emphasises the importance of evaluating CPD activity, including supervisory experiences, by reference to outcomes for service users and the development of the service (HCPC, 2012). In other words, to be meaningful, practice development must be orientated towards user needs, and case management that generates clear objectives based on needs and clear care plans therefore has an important role. This means case management is the partner of practice development and anchors practice development to user outcomes. So it is perhaps important that we recognise that balance is necessary and that there is a range of different approaches to supervision, each of which has its own strengths and weaknesses.

CASE STUDY 3.1

I reckon I've pretty much experienced every type of supervision in the known universe. I was supervised by a practice teacher when I was unqualified and the focus was on my learning and development, then in the general hospital I was 'theraped' – it was all about my feelings and the emotional responses of patients and personal growth. Don't get me wrong, it was useful stuff, just a bit odd. I had a flirtation with group supervision in a community team where we presented cases then a period in a psychiatric hospital where care planning was done in ward meetings supervised by the consultant. Now in Children's Services it is mostly case and risk management with a burst of wrist slapping performance management when my assessments are late.

There is a danger that the result of the professional versus managerial debate is that we lurch now to a new emphasis on professionalism and practice development only to lurch back in a few years, possibly after another scandal, to more effective case management. A key feature of public service could well be that, on an everyday basis, we have to grapple with and manage contradictions and paradox that cannot be handled if we adopt polarised positions. One of the skills that public service managers develop is perhaps the ability to manage paradox and negotiate a way between these polarised positions which can stop change and improvement and generate ineffectiveness (Dixon and Dogan, 2003).

Barry Johnson (1996), an important writer on polarity management, suggests that managers who can avoid getting stuck in one of these polarities perhaps hold the secret of effective management. Such a manager must be able to hold at the same time what can seem incompatible ideas, accepting their validity and perhaps their interconnectedness. They must be able to see the positive dynamics that can stem from the tension between polarities and find ways forward that make the best of what can be seen equally as valid perspectives or positions.

As an aid to polarity management, Johnson suggests the use of polarity mapping. In polarity mapping, having established the polarities they are grappling with, a manager then needs to highlight the 'upside' and the 'downside' of each of the polarities. This is helpful in reminding a manager of the nature and validity of both positions, but it also may open up a way forward in trying to avoid the downsides whilst mobilising the upsides of each polarity.

Table 3.1 is an example of a polarity map that perhaps demonstrates why we might seek to combine professionalism with managed services, and why grappling with the tensions between the two positions might be both necessary and productive.

Table 3.1 An example of a polarity map

UPSIDE	• flexible response to need; • personalised service; • high level of motivation and commitment; • potential for innovation; • expertise developed and mobilised to user's benefit.	• fair standardised services; • services open to public scrutiny; • good resource management; • co-ordination and collaboration is easier; • change can be centrally driven; • set procedures reduce risk to users.
POSITION	PROFESSIONAL AUTONOMY AND DEVELOPMENT	MANAGED APPROACH
DOWNSIDE	• non-standardised services and unfairness; • lack of transparency; • confusion over accountability; • can be a barrier to change; • can be a barrier to collaboration; • can increase risk to service users.	• lack of flexibility; • bureaucracy; • lack of a personalised response; • ill-thought out change; • shallow measures of performance; • can demotivate; • can limit innovation.

Something is achieved by perceiving the polarities and their dangers. It can help to find the balance that maintains the strengths from both positions and ameliorates the negatives.

However, what may also become apparent is the role of organisational power in this problem. Many of the negatives attributed to managerialism may be the result of an over-controlling approach, rather than management per se.

Power, authority and anti-oppressive practice in supervision

The definitions of supervision cited in Chapter 1 give an indication of the extent to which power is at the centre of the supervisory process, but do not necessarily pay much attention to it. The terms supervisor and supervisee demonstrate an implicit power imbalance, where one person with the knowledge and authority oversees the other. In contrast there is an aspiration for good supervision to be a collaborative venture, where both parties are enabled and empowered to work at their best to promote good outcomes for service users. Social work has a clearly developed analysis of oppression, and it would be naive to pretend that power dynamics are not influential within a supervisory relationship. Power is apparent, not only interpersonally, but also structurally, in the systems of the agency and institutions of wider society. To be able to develop a collaborative supervisory relationship, a discussion about the presence of power and anti-oppressive practice during the contract discussion is essential to ensure that these potentially difficult areas are acknowledged from the beginning.

The following bases of power, adapted from French and Raven's original model (Raven, 1992), are a useful way of considering the power of a supervisor.

1. **Legitimate power.** This is derived from the formal role or position held in the organisation. Sometimes referred to as '**authority**', it gives the person the right to require others to undertake tasks, make decisions and oversee work performance.

2. **Reward power.** This can also be referred to as **resource power** where the person has the ability to give or take away resources or rewards. Although in social work this is not usually associated with pay, it can be the power of controlling regrading or writing references. It can also mean gatekeeping, that is, controlling access to services and funding.

3. **Coercive power.** The ability to punish or reprimand someone for not undertaking tasks.

4. **Expert power.** This is based on the demonstrable knowledge and expertise that gives credibility to that individual.

5. **Referent power.** This can also be called **relational power** where power is gained by others seeing the person as being worthy of respect and wanting to be with them or like them.

6. **Information power.** Although it can be included in other bases, it is useful to separate it out to recognise the potency of being able to withhold or filter knowledge.

Another distinction which can be made when analysing power in supervision is to separate **formal power** derived through the organisation and including legitimate, coercive and reward power from **informal or personal power** which arises from the individual, and would be based in expertise and referent power.

Informal power not only includes individual expertise, but also derives from the individual personal and professional attributes. This then adds to the complexity of the analysis. Not only does consideration need to be given to personal characteristics but also issues of identity are important. Differences in ethnicity, class, gender, age, abilities and sexual orientation which have power dimensions defined at a societal and structural level will impact at the inter-personal level of supervision. Inequality of power, because of membership of the majority or a minority group, will compound an already complex situation. It requires an examination of the structural inequalities in the system and the power dynamics which can be created on an individual level. Non-oppressive supervision is reliant on a critical analysis about where power resides.

Brown and Bourne (1996) suggest that anti-oppressive practice in supervision needs to be based on an open and honest relationship where reflections on the power dynamics are regularly discussed. Trust will be built when each person has an understanding and acceptance of the other's perception of self and individual needs and strengths based on all of the dimensions of power outlined above.

The key to skilled and successful supervision is to use power effectively. Phillipson (2002) suggests that there are positive aspects to power and it can be very constructive to accept the appropriate use of authority when considering the management of work. A supervisor needs to be comfortable with the power that is legitimately derived from the role. The supervisee also needs to know that the supervisor is confident and able to utilise the power appropriately, and not fudge or sidestep the responsibility that comes with the authority. An empowering/anti-oppressive relationship is a cooperative relationship that acknowledges and honours difference. Further development can result in what Grimwood and Popplestone (1993, cited in Brown and Bourne, 1996) identify as collaborative power, which relies on all parties working together in a mutually supportive way to create innovation and change.

As we accept that power is multi-dimensional, it is also important to recognise the power of the supervisee. The less powerful member of any relationship can give or withhold their cooperation, and a reluctant or disgruntled supervisee can sabotage the task of supervision very successfully, either overtly or covertly. It is important for supervisors to be aware of this potential power and how it might be exercised to the detriment of supervision. For further discussion about how power might result in negative situations, see the section on resolving conflict and games in supervision (page 86). In contrast, an open honest relationship where differences in power are acknowledged and honoured and discussed right from the first meeting is the basis for a productive and rewarding supervisory relationship.

ACTIVITY **3.1**

Power and anti-oppressive practice

What power is the basis for your supervisory relationships? How comfortable are you with power? How do you use your power non-oppressively?

Identify two changes that would improve your anti-oppressive practice within supervision.

Leadership style and power

Another way of exploring power in supervision is through an exploration of leadership style. We would argue that three approaches to leadership combined together are crucial to ensuring that supervision is not over-controlling, and based on referent and expert power. They are:

- developmental leadership;
- ethical leadership;
- distributed leadership.

Developmental leadership

Developmental (sometimes called situational) approaches to supervision put forward the assertion that there are explicit stages that supervisees will move through to reach competence, and that they need distinct and different types of supervision dependent on their stage of development. By matching the need with a corresponding approach, supervision offers the right quantity and quality of support and direction. This demands flexibility from the supervisor as, through coaching and reflective practice, they enable the supervisee to increase their knowledge, skills and expertise.

Although it is doubtful whether all practitioners can be categorised so exactly, the approach does encourage a supervisor to consider the learning and supervisory needs of each supervisee and to focus on their development. Hersey and Blanchard's theory of situational leadership (Hersey and Blanchard, 1993) identifies four leadership styles that can be employed, dependent on how much support or direction is required (see Figure 3.1).

A more detailed application of this theory to supervision practice identifies four levels of a supervisee's professional maturity (Hawkins and Shohet, 2006; Loganbill *et al.*, 1982). The related supervisor approach is then expanded and offers specific strategies for each stage (see Table 3.2). The success of this model will depend on an accurate assessment of the supervisee's level of maturity in their role as well as the supervisor's ability to adapt to different needs.

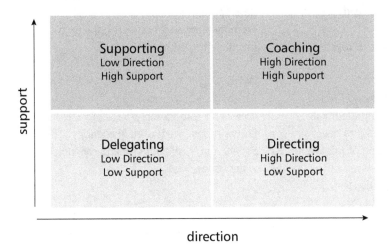

Figure 3.1 Situational leadership

Table 3.2 Supervisee's professional maturity and supervisor's approach

Supervisee's level of professional maturity	Supervisor's approach
Novice Staff member has little experience of task and is governed by rules and tasks. Is dependent on supervision for guidance and advice and can be anxious about completing role/task. Likely to over-focus on detail and content and sees tasks simplistically. Draws conclusions from discrete pieces of information, does not have a holistic approach.	**Directing** Provision of structure, teaching in formal and informal supervision. Offer regular and constructive feedback. Needs encouragement to reflect and learn new skills. Regular monitoring and observation.
Developing competence Staff member fluctuates between independence and dependence, and can sometimes be over-confident and other times overwhelmed. May sometimes blame supervisors for mistakes. Starting to engage with complexity. Starting to own the role and matching interventions to service user.	**Coaching** Will still need some structure and direction, but less than novice level. Supervision should allow time to reflect on own practice. Support and develop own style of working and independence. Allowance to make mistakes and learn from them. Focus on realities and wider context.
Competent practitioner Developing increased professional confidence and consistently able to perform tasks. Able to generalise about learning needs and skill development and sees wider context of service and user needs. Danger of boredom/habitual practice.	**Supporting** Supervision is more collaborative and discursive. Provision of new challenge and further development needed. Promote independence/responsibility to maintain interest in role.
Mature/expert Staff member has a significant level of professional maturity, integrated skills knowledge and awareness into deep professional understanding of role within organisation. Developed areas of expertise and able to help others learn skills. Awareness of own strengths and gaps.	**Delegating** Recognition of expertise. Give wider responsibility. Ensure experience is used in agency. Supervision is collaborative and can look at wider issues.

(Adapted from Morrison, 2005, and Hawkins and Shohet, 2006)

Whilst this model is useful, there can be a danger in applying it too rigidly and seeing each supervisee as fitting into the required developmental box without attention being paid to individual needs, the style of the supervisor and the uniqueness of the relationship. The complexity of the social work task can mean that supervisees can vary in their level of 'maturity' dependent on their current workload. It is also misleading to think of progression as linear, which can lead to considering any deviation from this path as dysfunctional. Supervisee development can be affected by various events and circumstances that can result in a perceived 'stand still' or the supervisee reaching a plateau. The importance of the approach is that it encourages the supervisor to think about the supervisee's needs and respond accordingly and means that they focus on developing the supervisee's practice.

A final point worth making is about the last 'stage' of mature/expert practitioner. Sometimes this can lead to too much autonomy and less frequent supervision, particularly in time pressured environments. This can result in supervisor and supervisee not being in regular communication with each other and can result in unsafe and unreflective practice. Also, the idea that a practitioner has somehow 'arrived' and no further practice development is possible or necessary is also unhelpful. Whilst more expert practitioners might need less supervision, regular supervision is still crucial. Rather, a collaborative relationship with experienced practitioners can be seen as allowing a better quality of supervision, and supervision allowing for learning and development across the whole of professional life, to the benefit of both supervisee and supervisor.

Crucially it is also worth noting that in developing the capability of individual supervisees and giving them more discretion, the supervisor gives up some power. As discussed in the section in the previous chapter on group supervision, there may be a storming period in a supervisory relationship where a supervisee challenges the supervisor. How you respond to challenge is therefore important. If you suppress it, the supervisory relationship and your supervisee's practice will not develop (see Chapter 5).

REFLECTION POINT

Thinking about the people you supervise; are you able to identify different levels of professional maturity? Are you a developmental leader offering each supervisee a different approach according to their needs?

Have your supervisees developed their professional maturity over the period in which you have been supervising them? What has helped them do so or what might be getting in the way? How do you handle challenges constructively?

Ethical leadership and supervision

Social work has a clear value base and codes of practice, which should be even more central to the supervision and leadership role than organisational policy and imperatives. Supervisors as leaders of teams could be seen to have a moral responsibility to use their authority to ensure everyone, including themselves, works within an ethical and value driven framework. In our experience, a value driven approach to supervision and practice is a good source of referent power and, apart from engaging supervisees, also motivates many supervisors. So an exploration of some of the writings on ethical leadership can be useful.

Heifetz (1994) suggests that leaders must use their authority to encourage people to respond to situations that have no easy answers, such as complex situations where there are conflicts of interest or perspective. The supervisor has a moral responsibility to face the issue and offer support for the supervisees to manage and confront difficult situations. They must also seek to counter avoidance and blaming behaviour in the process. The supervisor needs to be realistic about the personal and social costs of change, whilst maintaining a hopeful and optimistic perspective. Such an approach would seem essential in a supervisor but might also be seen as essential to a social worker in working with service users.

Yukl (2006) develops a framework for judging leadership behaviour and for developing ethical behaviour and an ethical culture in a team (see Table 3.3).

Table 3.3 Framework for judging leadership behaviour

Promoting an ethical climate	Opposing unethical practices
• Set an example of ethical behaviour by your own actions.	• Refuse to share in the benefits provided by unethical activities.
• Facilitate the development and dissemination of a code of ethical conduct.	• Refuse to accept assignments that involve unethical activities.
• Initiate discussions with followers or colleagues about ethics and integrity.	• Try to discourage unethical actions by others.
• Recognise and reward ethical behaviour by others.	• Speak out publicly against unethical or unfair policies in the organisation.
• Take personal risks to advocate moral solutions to problems.	• Oppose unethical decisions and seek to get them reversed.
• Help others find fair and ethical solutions to conflicts.	• Inform proper authorities about dangerous products or harmful practices.
• Initiate support services (e.g. ethics hotline, online advisory group).	• Provide assistance to others who oppose unethical decisions or practices.

(Yukl, 2006: 425)

This is a very demanding agenda for a supervisor and, whilst many of the supervisors we work with see ethical leadership as crucial to their practice, it creates considerable dilemmas for them. In particular many organisations are not very tolerant of criticism and there is perhaps an understandable reluctance to challenge organisational practices (SCIE, 2012b).

REFLECTION POINT

To what extent do you see yourself as an ethical supervisor?

How do you try and develop an ethical culture in your team?

What two actions or behaviours could you commit to that will enhance your ethical leadership?

To what extent do you feel empowered to challenge organisational practices? What are the pros and cons of confrontation?

Fairness and leader–member exchange theory (LMX)

A dimension of ethical leadership is 'fairness' in supervising your team. Being seen to behave unreasonably or to have favourites will undermine the team's trust in you. However, it is possible that the very act of leading a team can too readily generate unfairness almost as a natural team dynamic. Leader–member exchange theory (Yukl, 2006, and Graen and Cashman, 1975) focuses on the relationship between leaders and subordinates, suggesting that leaders have a different relationship with each individual. However, in contrast to Hersey and Blanchard's situational leadership, the relationship is not managed by the leader but is based on an exchange: the follower is actively engaged in the relationship as a two way process. The theory suggests that there are high- and low-exchange relationships, that is, different degrees of shared engagement. High-exchange relationships only occur with a few subordinates who, in effect, form a cadre of assistants or lieutenants who greatly facilitate the leader's team leadership.

The relationship develops over time and is based on mutual reward and it can too easily become a dependency for both parties. Personal attraction and compatibility provides the basis for the relationship and the use of coercion and authority by the leader can easily undermine it.

In contrast to high-exchange relationships, low-exchange relationships are confined to basic working relationships and contractual arrangements, that is, people work to job descriptions and in return receive salary and normal benefits: they are not privileged. However, it should be noted that low-exchange members are also not expected to play a more demanding role. High-exchange relationships are perhaps developed in stages, starting with a low-exchange relationship which develops over time as people get to know each other, find common ground, can judge performance, identify common attitudes and find compatibility. Shared interaction and tasks also serve to build trust and personal understanding and develop shared meaning so supervision becomes a ready means to building a high-exchange relationship.

Table 3.4 Leader and subordinate roles

Leader provides	Subordinate provides
Increased responsibility and authority	More work and dedication
Financial rewards and support for promotion	Personal support and loyalty
The best tasks	Shares the leader's tasks and responsibilities
More personal contact	Information and viewpoints
Confidences and privileged information	A sounding board
Freedom	Advocacy with other subordinates and a subordinate role model
Praise and encouragement	Praise and encouragement

(Based on Yukl, 2006)

High-exchange relationships can be seen as essential to a leader in that they provide them with support, information and feedback, a means to influence the wider team and the opportunity to delegate. In supervision they can be a source of energy, motivating both supervisor and supervisee and giving them increased satisfaction from their work and a bit of a buzz. However, they also have negative attributes and effects.

Unfortunately, there is some evidence that leaders tend to see subordinates engaged in a high-exchange relationship as succeeding through their own merits and failing only because of external factors, whilst low-exchange subordinates are seen to succeed through external factors and the help they receive and failing by their own efforts, or lack of them. The performance of high-exchange subordinates may also be subject to less scrutiny by the leader and the response to poor performance can be less punitive (Yukl, 2006).

Apart from meaning that performance of the team is not managed effectively, the impact of the unfairness on the motivation of low-exchange subordinates and, therefore, on their performance can be considerable and they can become a team resource that is not properly made use of or developed. In other words, your supervision can actually generate performance problems. Also, in contrast to good delegation and supervisory practice, it can mean that less effective team members get less leader time than they need. In contrast, the more able but also more favoured high-exchange subordinates get more leader time and attention.

The problem is that developing high-exchange relationships is seductive for a leader in the satisfaction it can provide and can be seen as essential in leading a team, almost a natural way to behave in order to lead effectively. However, the cost can be considerable and they readily undermine equal opportunities. For instance, a colleague pointed out to us how hard it is to build high-exchange relationships if you are a woman with a family and working part time.

Good performance management therefore becomes an important feature of leadership, so ironically we can end up seeing appraisal and performance measures, often identified as negative features of managerialism, as positively assisting leadership and supervision. So, for instance, clarity of practice standards and performance measures, methodical evidence gathering, the provision of regular supervision and appraisal opportunities for all staff working to a set format can all be seen as essential organisational features that support good leadership and supervision.

Beyond method, however, is an ethical and personal dimension. You must actively seek and be seen to be fair and sometimes this can be a considerable loss to you (see Case Study 3.2).

CASE STUDY 3.2

- *One of my supervisees out of nowhere suddenly became upset in supervision. She said that I was building a close relationship with a colleague and that she felt left out. She said that as a woman it was also hard to build a 'mates together' relationship like two men could. She was right and I had no choice but to pull back and make sure I was more even handed. I felt I missed out though on a rewarding and developing friendship that I had to put on hold.*

- *I can understand that it was an important way of him dealing with his stress but the little gang he had a fag with in the car park were a real clique. Sometimes he forgot that things he had discussed over a smoke he hadn't shared with the rest of us. Some of us felt very excluded from his small but unhealthy in-crowd.*

REFLECTION POINT

In your practice have you developed high-exchange relationships with some supervisees?

What might you do to be fairer as a leader and supervisor?

Distributed or participative leadership

Another very valuable leadership theory that, alongside situational leadership and ethical leadership, can mitigate against the misuse of power and an over-controlling approach is distributed or participative leadership. This involves mobilising the team as leaders making full use of their energy and expertise and empowering them to participate in leading the team with you.

Harris (2004), in a case study of the implementation of distributed leadership in a school, identifies a number of features:

- draws on expertise across the organisation;

- it builds organisational capacity;

- the formal leader's role is to 'hold the pieces of the organisation together in a productive relationship', i.e. a common goal or culture;

- distributed leaders are empowering, they help develop a clear sense of direction, build alliances, are inspiring, build confidence and self-esteem, and are a professional role model. They also reach out beyond the organisation to broader networks, mobilising them;

- techniques used included involving others in decision-making, delegation, rotating chairs, supporting staff-led initiatives, a team approach building collective responsibility.

Distributed leadership is particularly appropriate in professionalised organisations as it is in accord with the responsibility professionals have to lead and develop services. It is, therefore, a useful leadership model for social work. As suggested in the previous chapter, the quality of supervision is dependent on and supports the wider organisation and the service, so involving staff in the general leadership of the service can have a positive effect on supervision. Also, as discussed in the previous chapter, they can play an equal role in managing supervision, and in Chapter 7 we will explore how they can be engaged and contribute to developing supervision.

How do you know if you have distributed leadership in your team?

Distributed leadership has become very popular in exploring leadership in schools (National College for School Leadership (NCSL), 2011) and from this research it is possible to identify the features of an organisation with distributed leadership. We have developed a simple audit tool based on this research (Table 3.5) which identifies the features of distributed leadership.

Table 3.5 Features of distributed leadership

Attribute	Rating
Staff are actively involved in developing and evaluating policy and direction.	
Staff are participants in important decision-making.	
There is a shared vision among staff as to where they are going.	
Staff members have a commitment to the whole organisation as well as to their team.	
There is effective communication between management and staff and information is shared.	
Staff see the development/business plan as their own creation.	
Staff are willing to take on responsibility for improving what happens and come up with ideas that are then implemented.	
Staff take responsibility for intervening when they see something which runs against policy or vision.	
Formal training provides opportunities for staff to develop leadership and management skills.	
A wide range of staff at different levels have management and leadership roles (e.g. chairing a committee or working party).	
There is a sense of shared leadership among staff.	

An interesting feature of distributed leadership is the question of to what extent leadership can be distributed not only to staff but to people who use services. This can be seen as the principle behind co-production and personalised budgets, and we will discuss the involvement of people who use services in improving supervision in Chapter 7.

Distributed leadership can also be usefully used in combination with situational leadership which was discussed earlier in this chapter: a feature of professional maturity will be the contribution a professional makes to leading and developing the service. A team leader will seek to develop individuals and the effectiveness of the team as a whole, to facilitate distributed leadership.

Remember though, as in the discussion of situational leadership, distributed leadership means that a designated leader necessarily gives up power and they can be subject to uncomfortable challenges from the team as they try to develop a distributed approach. As with situational leadership, how you respond to challenge will either encourage the development of the team or block it.

REFLECTION POINT

With reference to the audit above have you achieved distributed leadership in your team?

Is there a distinction between your team and the wider organisation?

What might you do to develop distributed leadership? What might the barriers be?

Section 2
Relational aspects

In the last section we considered some of the objective and fundamental concepts of super-vision. This section now moves to looking at the relationships that underpin the task. In Chapter 4 we start with looking at self, and recognising that effective supervision depends on a supervisor who is able to manage self. Chapter 5 will then consider the 'other' in the supervisory relationship and how to build mutual understanding and make effective interventions in the relationship. Finally, in Chapter 6 we will look at strategies to resolve any difficulties that might arise in the working relationship. Underpinning this section will be the model of emotional intelligence referred to in the Introduction.

Chapter 4

The management and leadership of 'self' in supervision

. . . the only thing one can be sure of changing is oneself.

Aldous Huxley

Awareness of self as a supervisor

Within supervision, as well as all areas of social work, personal self-awareness is at least as important as knowing 'what to do' and 'how to do it' (Harrison and Ruch, 2007). As Shulman (1999, cited in Morrison, 2007) points out, a social worker can only really understand and be in touch with the feelings of those he or she works with if they have the ability to acknowledge their own emotions – in other words, are self-aware. So in supervision the same is true – as a supervisor, how much have you really thought about the role and impact of what you bring to supervision?

Goleman (1996: 46) defines self-awareness as a 'sense of an ongoing attention to one's internal states'. As a rule of thumb we are aware that how we feel influences how we react, but neurolinguistic programming (NLP) has added to our understanding by adding a level of detail that we think helps us to understand our internal processes in more depth. Their communication model looks at how we process the external world, how that affects our emotional state, and consequently how that affects our interaction with the external world.

It is well known that we need to filter the thousands of pieces of information that bombard us every second of the day. This is a survival strategy that allows us to function in the world. However, the filters used at any one time are unique to each individual, are how we make sense of the outside world, and result in features being 'altered' or edited before reaching the storage area of the brain.

Figure 4.1 illustrates how one piece of data becomes the representation in your mind, by passing through the filters as well as being influenced by our emotional and physiological state. The result is a very individual and unique internal representation of the event, which will then drive our behaviour or reaction.

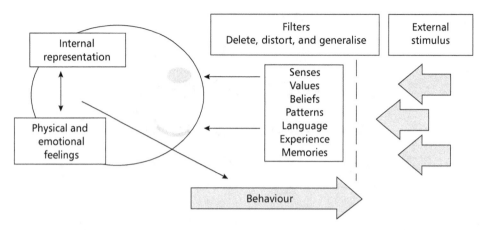

Figure 4.1 Internal communication model (based on James and Woodsmall, 1988, cited in Henwood and Lister, 2007)

What are the filters? Our senses, values and beliefs, patterns, language, experience and memories are all filters.

Senses: We take information through our unique visual, auditory, kinaesthetic, olfactory (smell) and gustatory (taste) systems.

Values, beliefs, preferences, experiences and memories: These are all filters which we apply in interpreting an event. Sometimes we are more aware of this process than others.

Language: Even if there is an agreement that the language is English, our individual use and understanding of words can be very different. The same word can have various meanings and interpretations, dependent on context. For example, think of how many ways you might interpret the word 'sensitive'.

We filter information about the world which results in internal representations or our own perceptions (reality) and this drives our behaviours and often reinforces a belief that our perception of the world is correct. So if your view of a supervisee is she is not organised, you will 'filter' for information to back up that belief and tend to ignore information that would disprove it.

How we filter: the process of deletion, distortion and generalisation

Deletion: We delete much of the information that is available to us. Research has shown that the conscious mind can only handle 7+/–2 pieces of information at any one time and yet our sensory receptors are actively processing millions of perceptions each second (Miller, 1956, cited in Doherty and Thompson, 2007). So our conscious mind learns to focus, and the information is selected through the filters we apply subconsciously. For example, remember when you have been in a noisy room and someone has said your name; you hear that voice, which you have previously ignored, above all the other sounds.

Distortion: This is the process by which we change the experience of the external world to make our own 'truth'. Psychological research has shown that people's recollections of car accidents are often very different to the actual event (Gross, 1996). For example, we attribute meaning to behaviours such as: *your supervisee postpones supervision three times in succession, and you interpret this as reluctance to engage*. This then can become a truth in your mind.

Generalisation: This is the basis of learning and we unconsciously look for links between experiences to draw conclusions and develop our understanding. This is similar to an understanding of stereotyping and involves jumping to conclusions based on previous experiences. For example you might conclude *that all new qualified social workers know nothing about the eligibility criteria* because the last two that you met didn't.

Impact of emotions and physiology

The final stages in this process of making sense and reacting to the world is the interaction of our emotional and physiological state. Our interpretation of the merest nod of the head can be different if we are feeling low, or even if we are hungry or have backache.

The result of this instantaneous yet complicated and mostly unconscious process is our unique reaction and behaviour to a particular event.

The benefit of this model is to give us a greater understanding of our own filters and patterns; how they affect what I see, feel and hear, and therefore how I react. Knowing this can then give us the opportunity to change and gain flexibility. It also means that we can understand someone else's filters and patterns and so will be better able to build rapport, and motivate them.

What we bring to supervision

Your personal and professional identity, including your own experience of supervision, brings a distinctive and unique approach to the situation. Negative and positive incidents within a supervisory relationship will impact on your capacity and confidence to be a supervisor. Other professional and organisational experiences will also influence and shape your behaviours and approach. It is also important to consider your own personal world and how that may affect your supervision style and attitude.

Taking time to consider what you bring to the supervision context can be a valuable way of preparing for the supervisory role.

It can also be a very worthwhile exercise as your supervisee will also be bringing their own and different 'history' and attitudes to the supervisory relationship.

Below is an exercise that gives a framework to reflect on your experiences and consider what constitutes your unique perspective in supervision.

ACTIVITY 4.1

Your experiences of supervision

Reflect on the following and note your answers to the questions:

1. *Your supervision history and relevant experiences*
   (a) *List your previous supervision/managerial experiences*
   (b) *What factors about these experiences were positive for you?*
   (c) *What factors or characteristics didn't you like?*
   (d) *What are your thoughts and feelings now, and how might they influence you?*

2. *Your personal and professional characteristics*
   (a) *What personal attitudes do you bring to supervision?*
   (b) *What are your strengths?*
   (c) *What areas do you need to work on?*
   (d) *What are your professional interests and plans?*

3. *From the questions above, write a few sentences that summarise your approach to supervision.*

This exercise is adapted from Morrison (2007: 92) and Davys and Beddoe (2010: 50).

Essential qualities and skills of a supervisor

The ability to be a good supervisor is more than just knowing or having experienced supervision. It is a skill based and relational activity and so demands a high level of interpersonal skills. It may be just stating the obvious, but these basic skills are at the heart of a good supervisory relationship, which has the core conditions of trust and safety.

Before embarking on a (new) supervision relationship, it can be well worth spending time preparing and planning the sessions and thinking about what skills you will need to use to facilitate this relationship.

Inventories of essential qualities are used in some supervision literature to throw light on the range of personal attributes and skills needed to be an effective supervisor. They can also act as a guide when considering your development needs. Their limitation is to see the list as complete or prescriptive. It is also important to recognise that possession of the qualities is rarely a clear cut yes or no, but more a work in progress. Table 4.1 demonstrates the breadth of qualities identified in the literature and as you will recognise many of the characteristics are already evident in your role as a competent practitioner.

Table 4.1 The essential qualities and skills of a supervisor

Hawkins and Shohet (2006: 50)	Davys and Beddoe (2010: 52)
1. Working map of the discipline	1. Competence and knowledge as practitioner
2. Flexibility in using concepts and models	
3. A multi-perspective view	2. Competence and training as supervisor
4. Capacity to manage and contain anxiety	3. Ability to challenge in a supportive manner
5. Openness to learning	
6. Ability to work transculturally	4. Openness to feedback and ability to be self-monitoring
7. Sensitivity to wider contextual issues	
8. Can handle power appropriately and non-oppressively	5. Ability to manage power and authority
9. Humour, humility and patience	6. Received and valued own supervision

In addition we would add the basic skills of:

1. listening and attending;
2. paraphrasing/summarising/clarifying/ prompting/probing/reframing;
3. questioning;
4. giving and receiving feedback;
5. use of silence;
6. assertiveness;
7. record-keeping.

ACTIVITY 4.2

The qualities of a supervisor

- Consider the lists above and decide if you would make any additions or deletions.

- Construct your own list of the most important eight qualities of a supervisor.

- Rate your own practice on a scale of 1 (high) to 5 (needing major development).

- Take two of the qualities you need to develop further.

- Decide on three or four steps that will help you make progress.

Transformational leadership: lessons for supervision

The literature on transformational leadership and more recently the work by Alban-Metcalfe and Alimo-Metcalfe (2009) about engaging leadership is helpful in looking at the qualities required for supervisors.

The original theory by Bass (1985) contrasted transactional and transformational leadership.

Transactional leadership is the model of leadership from a more predictable and stable social and political environment. It is clearly hierarchical and is simply concerned with performance. 'Subordinates' understand the expectations of their role, with rewards or punishments meted out dependent on the results.

Transformational leadership, on the other hand, is more complex and focuses not simply on performance measures. It is concerned with developing employees to reach their full potential, encouraging them to go beyond self-interest and accept a group vision or mission. By behaving in a transformational way, the leader is able to build a team of hard working and motivated workers who will be committed to improving their performance. It is a more flexible approach and more suited to the modern, more complex work environment where change and diversity are important characteristics.

The research by Alimo-Metcalfe *et al.* (2008) investigated the impact of transformational leadership on organisational performance in the NHS. They found that transformational or 'engaging' leadership increases levels of staff motivation, satisfaction and commitment. It also had a noticeable effect on reducing stress and emotional exhaustion and increasing general team effectiveness and productivity.

Govier and Nash (2009) summarised an 'engaging leader' as someone who is focused on enabling and empowering others, as well as a remarkable motivation to get the work done. They have strong personal qualities of openness and honesty, combined with humility. The emphasis of engaging leadership is on serving and enabling others to display leadership themselves. The model emphasises the importance of collaborative team work, and valuing everyone's contribution towards achieving the organisational goals.

Defining the characteristics of a transformational leader can be a useful framework for considering your own practice. Alimo-Metcalfe and Alban-Metcalfe (2001) identify nine factors that are present in transformational leaders in the UK.

1. Genuine concern for others

The leader has a genuine interest in the follower as an individual and develops their strengths.

2. Political sensitivity and skills

The leader is sensitive to the political pressures that politicians face; understands the political dynamics of the leading group; can work with elected members to achieve results.

3. Decisiveness, determination, self-confidence

The leader is decisive when required; prepared to take difficult decisions; self-confident; resilient to setbacks.

4. Integrity, trustworthy, honest and open

The leader makes it easy for the follower to admit mistakes; is trustworthy; takes decisions based on moral and ethical principles.

5. Empowers, develops potential

The leader trusts the follower to take decisions/initiatives on important issues; delegates effectively; enables individuals to fully develop their potential.

6. Inspirational networker and promoter

The leader has a wide network of links to the external environment; effectively promotes the work/achievements of the department/organisation to the outside world; is able to communicate effectively the vision of the authority/department to the public/community.

7. Accessible, approachable

The leader is accessible to staff at all levels; keeps in touch using face-to-face communication.

8. Clarifies boundaries, involves others in decisions

The leader defines boundaries of responsibility; involves staff when making decisions; keeps people informed of what is going on.

9. Encourages critical and strategic thinking

The leader encourages the questioning of traditional approaches to the job; encourages people to think of wholly new approaches/solutions to problems; encourages strategic, rather than short-term, thinking.

ACTIVITY **4.3**

Assessing leadership skills

Think of someone who you consider to be a good leader and supervisor. Using the nine factors above – what do they do well?

Think of your own leadership and supervisory practice. Which of these behaviours do you demonstrate well?

Which are your weaker areas?

Self-management and personal leadership in supervision

The second dimension of emotional intelligence referred to in the Introduction is self- or emotional management (Goleman, 1996). A useful definition is provided by Mills and Domeck (2005):

> *Emotional management involves your ability to control the feelings you express so that they remain appropriate to a given situation. Becoming skilful at emotional management requires that you cultivate skills such as maintaining perspective, being able to calm yourself down, and being able to shake off out-of-control anxiety, or sadness.*

From the discussion about the NLP communication model (on page 48), it is clear that there is a close relationship between our emotions, physiology, external stimulus and our reactions and behaviours. However, the essence of emotional management is to recognise that behaviour may be provoked in an individual by external events and actions, but it is not ultimately determined by them. In other words, you have a choice about how you will react to any given situation. Nothing or no one 'makes' you do something!

A more proactive view of self-management is not just about reacting to events, but to be creating and leading your own actions. Stephen Covey, who talks about 'self mastery' in his seminal work *The 7 Habits of Highly Effective People* (Covey, 2004), identifies the strategies, behaviours and attitudes used by successful people and synthesises this into seven 'habits'.

The strategies in the following sections can be used to develop your personal leadership practice.

Outcome thinking

Many organisational behaviour and leadership books will talk of goals and targets, and this is increasingly the language of social care. SMART (specific, measurable, achievable, realistic and timed) is used to set appropriate goals. However, there is an important first stage before this. Covey thinks that all actions or goals should 'begin with the end in mind' (2004: 95). All dreams and visions are first created in your mind, and spending time getting clarity about what it is that you want to achieve is vital before the next step of manifesting it in reality, when targets and goals can be set.

NLP thinkers (O'Connor, 2001: 13; Knight, 2009: 240) add that much of the way we think is from a problem perspective, that is, what is it that we don't want. This often results in a 'fire fighting' approach and a focus on the problem. Success is about developing a clear and compelling vision of what it is you want to do, and is called 'outcome thinking'.

CASE STUDY *4.1*

Neela is constantly busy, but not feeling that she is getting anywhere. She is managing a busy children's assessment team and has been there for two years. When asked what she wants to do, she talks about wanting to 'get out of the pressurised workplace'. She looks for jobs in many different sectors and says she is open to anything, but nothing ever seems to be right.

Aman is constantly busy, but not feeling that he is getting anywhere. He is managing a busy children's assessment team and has been there for two years. When asked what he wants to do, he says he recognises the skills he has developed and now wants to work more directly with children. He is considering work in more specialist teams.

REFLECTION POINT

Who is more likely to make a successful move to another job, Neela or Aman?

Outcome thinking is therefore having a clear idea of what you want. NLP has a useful model for setting outcomes that are 'well-formed', that is, likely to be successful. The steps and questions can be used to think about long-term outcomes, such as your career journey or life purpose, or more short-term objectives, such as chairing a difficult meeting successfully.

So, let's consider applying the model to your vision for supervision.

Step 1 is to think about what you want. This sometimes means reconsidering what you see as a problem and thinking about what would be the best outcome in the situation. So the statement is then framed as a positive statement. To use words that express what the future will be brings energy and motivation to the task. To help to get to this point, it may help to reflect on what the real issue is and what is really important about achieving this outcome.

For example:

> *Chris is a new supervisor, working in a busy assessment team. The problem is that within the organisation, supervision does not seem to be valued; sessions are often cancelled, cut short or focus only on urgent issues. She thinks that supervision is really key to good practice and wants to promote excellent supervisory practice, but she is worried she will become like everyone else. Thinking it through positively Chris decides that her outcome is: 'I want to be an excellent supervisor'.*

Step 2 is working out the context in which you want to achieve this outcome. This encourages you to be specific about when, where, who with and so on.

Chris thinks about this and decides that the context is within her team and with her supervisees. She also decides that 12 months is a good period of time to work with.

Step 3 is knowing when you have succeeded. What will be the evidence? This encourages you to be really specific about your outcome, and you know what you will see, feel, hear, when you have achieved it.

> *Chris takes some time to imagine what it will be like to be an excellent supervisor. She realises that her evidence will be seeing herself attending and listening to the supervisees and noticing that they are enjoying the supervision sessions. She will be able to look back over the year and know that everyone has had regular uninterrupted supervision time, with space to talk about all aspects of work and professional development. She will hear good reflective discussion in supervision sessions, and she will feel positive and confident about her role as a supervisor. In the supervision reviews, her supervisees will say the relationship has been supportive, empowering and challenging.*

Step 4 is considering the internal and external resources you need to achieve your outcome, and importantly that they are within your control. (If your outcome is dependent on winning the lottery, it may need rethinking!). Internal resources to consider are personal skills, commitment and energy. External resources may be money, organisational time and other people's support.

> *Chris knows that she has the internal resources of skill, commitment and energy, but knows she needs to talk with the management team to get their support to find the time and space for uninterrupted one-to-one time. She decides to put it to a meeting as a project that can be reviewed and evaluated. She knows she has control over her inner resources but that the external support is an area she may need to revisit during the year.*

Step 5 is considering the ecology of the outcome, that is, the wider systemic consequences. Who or what 'in the system' might be affected by this change, positively and negatively?

> *Chris knows that good supervision has been shown to improve work practices and practitioners' confidence, but that in the short term finding the time may mean extra*

pressure on duty when supervision is taking place. She talks with the team to work out how best this can be handled, which results in decisions about when and where supervision sessions are best held.

Step 6 is considering what is good about the present situation or what you will have to give up that will stop you achieving your outcome (secondary gain). This is important as it can be the overlooked area, and can take some honesty to acknowledge what is preferable about 'how it is'.

Chris reflects on her secondary gain and recognises that it would be less work and easier to go with the present situation and be able to blame external forces for not being a good supervisor. Here she is taking a risk and knows that it will need her to be strong and well-organised. Having thought it through, she is clear that achieving her outcome is much more compelling than the present situation.

Step 7 is the desirability check, and is the review to be sure that, having considered all the questions, the outcome is well-formed, or needs modifying. It is also the time to re-check, to make sure it fits in with your values and long-term vision of your life plan.

Chris spends some time comparing her outcome to her personal values and to what she thinks she wants to do in the long term. She knows she likes the team and area of work and wants to stay in that workplace. She is clearer about the specifics of what being an excellent supervisor is and feels it is a good match with what her values are.

Step 8 is deciding on the action plan and taking the first step. The process so far is about setting the outcome – only now is the time to work out the action plan and then most importantly take the first step. Use of SMART objectives can be useful at this stage.

Chris's action plan involves making the supervision arrangements, deciding when to draft contracts, sending supervisees requests to meet, working out protocols for recording, thinking about models for reflection.

Her first step is to set up a meeting with her team to talk through the plan and diarise first meeting times.

To summarise, these are the questions to ask to set a well-formed outcome:

1. **What do you want?**

State your outcome in the positive. Make it as detailed as possible; think about why it is important.

2. **What is the context in which it will be achieved?**

When, where, who with, etc.

3. **Evidence**

How will you know when you have succeeded (or are on the right track)?

What will you see, hear and feel when you achieve it?

4. **Resources**

What are the internal and external resources you need to achieve your outcome? Are they in your control?

5. **How does this fit with the wider system? (In NLP this is called ecology)**

Who or what 'in the system' might be affected by this change, positively and negatively? Does it fit with your/others' values? What barriers might you will face and how will you get over these?

6. **What is good about the present situation that might cause resistance to change? (In NLP this is called secondary gain)**

Is the reward of achieving this outcome big enough to compensate you for the loss of how things are now?

7. **Desirability check**

Having got this far – do you really want the outcome? Does it fit with your values?

What changes would make it more desirable?

8. **Commit to the first step**

What specifically will you do? Make an action plan and take the first step.

A review process can be added to this model, using similar questions which can ensure the outcome stays on track or is modified appropriately. The well-formed outcome process can be used in all types of decision-making. The exercise sheet in Appendix 4 gives the step-by-step process to setting a well-formed outcome.

Put first things first: self-management not time management

Pressurised working environments and consequent lack of time is one of the major reasons put forward for irregular or inadequate supervision. Sessions, diarised for months, are often cancelled when other more urgent issues take precedence. The ability to commit the time for an effective session is summed up by Gould and Baldwin: 'fragile within an ever busy working environment' (2004: 16).

Covey (2004) offers a model (outlined in Table 4.2) as a way of helping to prioritise where your energy and resources need to be directed. He does not see it as a time management tool, but more about self-management.

The essence of the model is to recognise there are two factors that define any activity: level of importance and urgency. Urgent activities are there in front of you, pressing you to take action, such as a ringing phone or an unexpected visitor wanting to see you. Important activities are the ones that are related to results. Sometimes they are the bigger pieces of work, but these are the activities that will make the difference.

We react to urgent matters, but important tasks, particularly if they are not urgent, need proactivity.

Table 4.2 Managing time

	Urgent	Not urgent
High importance	**1. Quadrant of Demand (Daily Reality)** Crises Pressing problems Deadline projects Critical tasks	**2. Quadrant of Quality** Planning improvements Prevention planning Relationship building New opportunities/projects Self-development Develop and empower others (Supervision) Purposeful recreation
Low importance	**3. Quadrant of Illusion** Interruptions Some calls and mail Pressing matters without impact Popular activities Activities you feel obliged to do Some meetings	**4. Quadrant of Waste (Escape)** Trivia Time wasters Internet surfing Some phone calls Socialising/gossip

(Adapted from Covey, 2004)

Quadrant 1 is the most exhausting place to be, and 'burn out' in social work comes from spending most of your working day there. The consequences to health are obvious, and the only place anyone wants to go after a long time here is to Quadrant 4 or possibly 3, just to get some down time.

Quadrant 2 is the most productive use of work time, and is the heart of effective self-management. It includes the important and not urgent work which gets left behind but can produce more effective ways of working. The aim is to grow the amount of time you spend in Quadrant 2.

The aim of effective self-management is to spend most of your week in Quadrant 2, followed by Quadrant 1, then Quadrant 3 and lastly 4.

Rebalancing the workload will come from taking time from the activities of Quadrant 3 and 4, and, as you can see, they are the low-importance tasks. It may be difficult to shrink Quadrant 1 initially, but focusing on increasing the quality work of Quadrant 2 should limit the number of urgent demands.

ACTIVITY 4.4

Managing your time

Take some time to categorise your activities into the 4 quadrants.

Where do you spent most of the time in the working week? Give a rough percentage at the beginning of the week and then review at the end.

What could you do to spend more time in Quadrant 2?

Commit to setting a limit on the amount of time taken up by two activities or behaviours in Quadrant 3 or 4 to free up two hours of Quadrant 2 activity.

Promoting resilience in self (and supervisee)

Laming (2009) emphasised the need for social workers to develop emotional resilience. The concept of resilience is useful, as it goes beyond the traditional ideas of managing stress, and considers the more holistic perspective of wellbeing.

Munro (2011b) and Mor Barak *et al.* (2009) state that our ability to self-manage can be improved by using strategies developed to increase our emotional resilience, which in turn has been shown to provide some protection against the stress of social work.

In their recent study, Kinman and Grant (2011) found that developing skills of self-awareness and ability to understand others, particularly through reflection, was useful in building resilience.

Tugade and Frederickson (2004, cited in Collins 2007: 256) define psychological resilience as 'effective coping and adaptation when faced with hardship or adversity'. Collins (2007) says it can be characterised by an ability to 'bounce back' from negative emotional experiences. Resilient individuals are not rare, or exclusively positive – they will have negative emotions in the same way as less resilient people, but are not overwhelmed by them, and have developed strategies to offset their impact. As social workers and supervisors, we will encounter a range of negative emotions, and using strategies to develop resilience will improve our personal and professional life.

Research by Kobasa (1979) and Maddi *et al.* (1998) has resulted in the development of a model of hardiness or resilience based on evaluating the ability to handle and manage problems or difficulties. They propose that three characteristics are found in resilient people:

- Having a strong characteristic of *commitment* that will find ways to *see the positive in a situation* and remain involved. The person will have an active problem-solving approach and can find meaning in activities even when faced with significant adversity.

- Believing you have *control* over present circumstances enables the person to think they can influence the course of events, rather than being a victim of circumstance. This will enable them to 'hang in there' longer than someone who feels helpless.

- Control is differentiated into primary control (where there is the ability to change a situation positively) and secondary control (which is the ability to change how you think about a situation).

  ○ Secondary control can also be called 'reframing' and is a useful technique to practise. By changing how you perceive a situation, you can change the meaning and thereby change your response (for further information, see O'Connor, 2001).

- Enjoying *challenges* and so seeking out opportunities for continual growth and learning, rather than staying in routine and safe comfort zones. This proactive attitude sees stress more as a challenge that is neither unfair nor unfortunate, but part of life to be accepted and worked with. Combined with a realistic understanding of your own capabilities and limitations, it means challenges are at an appropriate level.

Developing resilience is important for the supervisor and the supervisee. Supervision is clearly a place where the supervisee can develop these strategies and you may consider what questions or interventions you can use to encourage this.

ACTIVITY **4.5**

Developing resilience in difficult situations

- **Commitment:** *Find ways to see the positives of a situation. What aspects can I commit to?*

- **Control:** *Believe you can influence events and not be a victim of circumstance.*

What can I do to influence/achieve the outcome?

How can I reframe this situation to regain a sense of perspective and control? What do I accept and what can I change?

- **Challenge:** *Seek out opportunities for growth; what is the opportunity for my learning in this situation? What positive steps can I take to develop the skills to work differently?*

Managing self in difficult situations

Highly charged situations can result in slow and muddled thinking, particularly if our emotions have been 'hijacked'. Neuroscience recognises the role of the part of the brain called the amygdala in triggering the fight or flight response if we feel under threat. Being able to practise some techniques to keep this arousal under control can be very helpful in supervision, and in everyday life.

Anchoring

This is a useful technique to develop positive self-management when faced with a difficult situation that triggers a negative emotional state. It is particularly useful when planning for a difficult meeting or court appearance.

An *anchor* is a stimulus that becomes a trigger to make us respond in a certain way. It can be visual, auditory, a feeling, a smell or a taste. Existing anchors can set off emotions by remembering a particular experience. For example, hearing the first three notes of your favourite piece of music can create a warm feeling inside as you remember not only the rest of the music, but also any associated memories. A picture of your family by your desk can evoke a sense of joy. Equally, anchors can be negative. Certain places, people, events can make us feel upset, sad or afraid. For instance, just the smell of perfume worn by a critical teacher can bring back negative memories. You may be unaware of many of these anchors – in other words, they operate at a subconscious level. We can use positive anchors to improve our ability to work in difficult circumstances, exercise more control over our behaviour and actions and achieve outcomes we are working towards.

The process

Find a quiet space where you will not be interrupted and you may need a pen and a blank piece of paper. Allow about 10 minutes.

- Step 1: Think about the situation you are preparing for and decide on the 'state' you want to be in. For example, you may write down 'confident' or 'assertive', but be specific about what sort of 'confident' or 'assertive' you mean. Add more precise words, so that you have a really comprehensive understanding.

- Step 2: Decide on the gesture or 'anchor' that you want to use. This needs to be easy to apply in the situation you want to use it and has to be distinct, in your control, short and easily repeatable. It can be visual, auditory or kinaesthetic. Hand gestures may work well, such as clenching your fist, pressing your first finger and thumb together or squeezing your wrist. Visual or auditory ones can include looking at a picture or repeating a particular word.

- Step 3: Think of a specific occasion when you remember being in the state you identified in Step 1. It must be a positive memory and you need to be central. Then spend a minute fully re-experiencing the situation. For example, think about the people who are also there and their movements and expressions; remember any colours, voices or other sounds. What were you doing, saying and thinking – such as, were you walking around or sitting down, talking or listening, what were you saying to yourself?

- Step 4: Then, when the memory is really strong – make the anchor or gesture you decided upon in Step 2, and hold it for a count of five. Let go and relax as your memory and feelings created in Step 3 start to diminish.

- Step 5: Then let go of that memory completely by doing something totally different for 20 seconds; perhaps stand up, turn around and sit down again, look around the room or remember what you ate at your last meal.

- Step 6: Repeat Steps 3, 4 and 5 at least three times to strengthen the anchor (to make that link between the internal emotional feeling and the external stimulus).

- Step 7: Now think of the next time you need to be in that positive state. As you imagine the situation, set (or 'fire') off your anchor and notice the intensity of the feelings that you experience, and how much more positive your responses are.

    It is possible to add even more positive states to this one anchor by identifying the state, then repeating Steps 3–6.

You should find that the more you build these anchors, the more you will be in control of your actions and feel positively able to achieve your goals.

(Adapted from Henwood and Lister, 2007)

In the moment techniques

Breathing: Focusing on your breath is a great way of calming yourself in a stressful situation, and a particular technique is to make the out breath longer than the in breath. This helps to release oxygen into your bloodstream and to your brain.

The in breath should be deep into the diaphragm for a count of about seven, relaxing the shoulders at the same time. The out breath should be for a count of about eleven. The actual time is less important than getting a ratio of approx 3:7.

Counting to 10: A very well known technique of doing something trivial, but cognitive, which engages the frontal cortex or thinking part of the brain and allows the amygdala trigger to quieten down.

Looking after yourself

Preserving and enhancing the greatest asset you have – you.

(Covey, 2004: 288)

To be effective at work [it] is vital to be constantly learning and attending to how we nourish and sustain all aspects of our being.

(Hawkins and Shohet, 2006: 16)

It is well known that working in social work and health care can drain energy and lead to burn out and stress. It is also well known that prevention is better than cure, so this section is not going to theorise but is a challenge to change your practice.

Hawkins and Shohet (2006) asked friends and colleagues who were 'flourishing' in their work to talk about how they achieved that state. Covey (2004) looks at the dimensions of self-renewal. Drawing on their conclusions here are six recommendations for resourcing and renewing yourself:

1. Enjoy learning. Stay at your learning edge and have a learning project.

2. Attend to your emotional wellbeing; plan activities that increase your 'feel good' factor.

3. Increase your capacity to relate to and engage others.

4. Attend to your physical wellbeing: diet, exercise, sleep, breaks.

5. Have a regular personal or spiritual practice.

6. Spend good quality time with a group of co-learners/good friends.

ACTIVITY **4.6**

Practical steps to managing difficult situations

Spend time considering each of the areas. What practical steps can you take to make a small but significant change?

What are your resource systems that can support you in your work and in making changes?

Chapter 5

The supervisory relationship

This chapter explores how we need to take into account the other person(s) and their characteristics and how we can build and manage effective supervisory relationships that are the foundations for effective supervision. Many of us will hold the belief that we are all different and unique, and difference is to be celebrated; however, the challenge can sometimes be to apply this to situations where we want to reach a mutual understanding.

Understanding the 'other' in supervision

Building a real understanding of how each person (including ourselves) perceives a situation can extend our insight and wisdom about the attitudes and behaviours we can adopt to reach a good solution.

You may have heard the saying that before you criticise someone, you need to walk a mile in their shoes. In other words, you can't really understand someone until you've experienced what it's like to be in their situation. The ability to see the other's point of view, often called 'empathy', is a key skill in understanding people and vital for good communication in any relationship, particularly supervision. Seden defines empathy as 'the capacity to enter into the feelings and experiences of another; to understand what the other is experiencing as if you were the other; to stand back from your own self and identity in the process' (2005: 74).

Despite our desire to empathise, it is not unusual to find ourselves puzzled by a supervisee's behaviour or perspective. It can be difficult to step back from our own viewpoint to 'imaginatively enter into the inner life of someone else' (Kadushin and Kadushin, 1997: 108).

A model drawn from NLP is a useful exercise that can help to gain that insight. Perceptual Positions, developed originally by Grinder and DeLozier (O'Connor, 2001), gives us a highly effective way of understanding any situation from different perspectives. It gives the opportunity to understand the dynamics of a relationship and bring a balanced appreciation of self and other.

It is particularly useful when resolving difficult issues, but it has wider uses; it can be used for preparing for meetings, giving presentations, writing reports, managing arguments – generally working with 'other people'.

A perceptual position is a perspective that includes feelings, beliefs, patterns and behaviours, as well as the information gathered from the sensory systems (mainly visual, auditory and kinaesthetic).

First position

The 'I' position, where you see the world from purely *your* own point of view and you accept your reality. What is it that you are seeing, hearing, feeling and thinking? What assumptions and filters are being applied (see communication model on page 48 for further explanation). It is important to be really honest.

Second position

The other person's position (sometimes thought of as standing in their shoes). You process the situation from the other person's view of the world. It is a creative leap of imagination and gives you the ability to appreciate the other person's perspective. You are finding out what the person is experiencing; seeing, hearing, feeling. You are associating with their reality. You understand their positive intention and the reason for their behaviour. It is really important to leave as much of the thoughts and feelings from the first position behind, in order to be fully able to associate with how that other person is understanding their world.

Third position

This is the 'fly on the wall' or observer position, where you are uninvolved and outside of the situation. It is a detached unemotional perspective. Here you leave behind all the thoughts and feelings generated by self and other and become a dissociated independent witness. You are able to examine both positions, and the relationship between them. From this vantage point you may notice some odd patterns or complex games that are often hidden from other perspectives.

By taking up all these three positions we are able to understand the positive intentions of all parties which are underlying their behaviour.

The essence of understanding someone else is having the flexibility to take up all three perceptual positions and use what you learn in your interactions. Sometimes people seem to be 'stuck' in one of the positions. A person who is only able to see the world from their point of view could be stuck in the first position and may be perceived as egotistical. A person who only seems to consider the view of the other person could be stuck in the second position and may

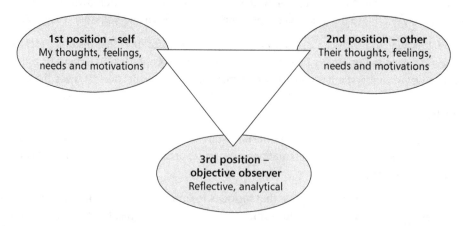

Figure 5.1 Perceptual positions

be perceived as a 'rescuer', who does not consider their own view as important. A person who seems to only analyse relationships and be detached and unaffected by emotions could be stuck in the third position and may be perceived as cold and unfeeling.

ACTIVITY **5.1**

Perceptual positions

In this exercise you will need to create three different physical spaces to be able to fully experience the three different positions. You can use chairs or just use the space in an office.

Step 1 *Move into space 1 – this is the first position.*

As yourself ask the following questions:

- *What is the issue and who is the other person?*

- *What are my best intentions for the situation and everyone involved?*

- *How am I feeling about the situation?*

- *What do I want to achieve here/what is my outcome?*

When you have gained a good understanding of this position, move away from that chair/space and do something to leave those emotional feelings in that space, for example, by remembering something neutral such as what you had for breakfast.

Step 2 *Move into space 2 – this is the second position: the other person's perspective.*

It can be useful to adopt the same posture and language as the other person to understand how they feel. It is important to believe that their present behaviour is the best way they know how to act in the present circumstances.

Answer these questions as if you are the other person:

- *How am I feeling about the situation?*

- *What do I think of the other person?*

- *What are my best intentions and what do I want/need from the situation?*

- *What will that give me?*

When you have gained a good understanding of this position, move away from that space and do something to leave those emotional feelings in that space, for example, by thinking about something neutral again.

Step 3 *Move into space 3 – this is the third position: the fly on the wall/independent perspective.*

Answer these questions as if you were detached, distant and an unemotional observer.

- *What do you notice about the different perspectives of each person?*

- *What do you notice about the relationship between these two people?*

ACTIVITY **5.1** *(CONT.)*

- *What could person A (you) do differently to improve the situation?*

- *Are there any other suggestions/advice for person A?*

When you have a good understanding of this position, go back to space 1.

Step 4 *Space 1: You are back as yourself.*

- *What differences do you notice about how you feel about the situation now?*

- *What new ideas and perspectives have you discovered?*

Take time to assimilate this new information and be aware of new feelings.

Step 5

- *What steps will you take to move the situation forward?*

- *When will you take these steps?*

It can be helpful to learn this technique by asking someone else to act as a facilitator or coach for the first few times. They can help to make sure that you move from each position 'cleanly' without bringing thoughts and feelings from one position into another.

Alternative exercise

It is also a good exercise to help a supervisee to work through a difficult situation. You can take on the role of a facilitator, ask them the questions, highlight when there may be contamination from another position, and help them process the answers.

Managing relationships

Rapport

Being able to build rapport is one of the most important skills in communicating effectively and being able to manage relationships. In essence it can be described as a relationship of mutual understanding, where there is respect and harmony between the participants. Kadushin and Kadushin suggest that rapport is when 'the participants are in tune with one another, in sync with each other' (1997: 101). When people are 'in rapport' you will notice that their body language is often matched; for example, they move 'in sync' with each other. They recognise and appreciate each other, emphasising the similarities and respecting differences. Their conversation is easy, and language and tone are often matched.

Establishing rapport is an important step to developing an effective supervisory relationship. It generates an environment where honest discussions about sensitive and difficult subjects can bring about realistic plans of action, that all are committed to.

Building rapport it is about building trust and confidence in each other, and is often something that we can do naturally and unconsciously. However, the skill is to be able to consciously construct a relationship with strong rapport, particularly if there is not a 'natural affinity'.

Developing rapport with anyone has to be predicated with having a genuine interest and curiosity about someone, and respecting their different views. A strategy to build rapport is:

1. To notice the other person's behaviour and communication patterns. There are many aspects that you could focus on:

   - Body language

   - Posture: Notice how the other person is standing, sitting, positioning their arms and legs, inclining their head. Do they seem relaxed or tense?

   - Movement: Notice the pace of the other person – are they fidgety or still? Do they move at a fast pace or slowly?

   - Breathing pattern: Is their breathing shallow, fast, deep, slow?

   - Voice: Notice the pace, volume and tone of the communication

   - Language: Notice the pattern of words used. Are they predominantly visual, auditory or kinaesthetic? Do they indicate which meta programme is preferred (see next section for further explanation)? Are there key words which indicate their values?

2. Be aware of the differences between their style and yours.

3. Modify your behaviours and physical movements to match theirs. Matching is not copying, which can be quite disrespectful and merely mimics someone else's behaviour. Matching is more like a dance and demands a skill in harmonising and adopting similar and complementary postures. It is about deeply noticing how someone moves or holds positions, and developing an awareness of who they are. It need only be matching the small movements, such as how they interlace their fingers, or hold their head to one side. Taking on a similar style can result in two effects: (a) the person unconsciously feels accepted and valued; and (b) you will also gain an understanding of who they are. It is a skill that demands subtlety and, like any skill, needs practice. You may be better at matching some aspects than others. It is worth concentrating on individual aspects such as the voice for a few days, and then notice if it is easier.

Once rapport is established you have created the environment for optimum communication. This gives you the opportunity to influence the other person. This is part of any supervisory relationship and perhaps the least discussed. This is possibly because it feels a little manipulative, although it is no different from other techniques we are taught and use to enhance an interaction. Another way of thinking about it is that it is a skill which eliminates a lack of harmony and accord that can get in the way of communication and shared reflection, so that it is ultimately empowering.

Recognising patterns and being able to influence others

We all have established patterns of behaviour that have developed through our life experiences, and the section about the internal communication model (page 48) recognised how this results in how we unconsciously filter information. Being aware of another person's patterns and matching them can really enhance rapport and communication. Knowledge of someone's 'meta programmes' is one way of recognising patterns. These 'habits of thought' can be identified by language patterns: the words that we use. Someone with a similar meta programme will use similar words, and so recognising significant words can help us to identify how someone is thinking. Charvet (1997) suggests that matching someone's meta pro-grammes by using similar language patterns will enable your message to be more fully understood and accepted by the other person.

This model can help supervisors/team leaders to notice and appreciate how a supervisee or colleague may understand and behave in a situation, and how it is similar or different from their own view. It also provides the tools to develop more effective relationships and to influence behaviour. In this way we may have more success in taking a leadership role and influencing people to agree to a particular course of action.

There are no 'right' and 'wrong' meta programmes. They are merely descriptions of patterns at a particular moment in time. They are context dependent and not 'personality traits'. We may often behave the same way in a particular environment, such as at work, but may be very different at home or with friends. This means that meta programmes are not a method of stereotyping people, but recognising a pattern of behaviour in similar contexts.

Meta programmes are more fully explored in Holroyd (2012), but here are three that are particularly relevant to supervision.

Internal/external

This meta programme deals with *where* does a person find motivation; how do they evaluate information to be able to take action? An *internal* person is self-motivated. They will evaluate information and their performance based on their own internal standards. They will gather information from others, or hear orders, but this is only information and they will decide on its relevance or accuracy. They need very little external praise, but also tend to not give much feedback. They have difficulty in accepting others' views and can be difficult to supervise. They will talk about their own performance and will often say 'I know'. They will resist being told what to do. The influencing language you can use to motivate an *internal* person are phrases like 'only you can decide', 'you might want to consider', 'this is a suggestion you could think about' and 'what do you think'.

An *external* person needs other people's views and direction to stay motivated. They need feedback to know how well they are performing, and can get demotivated without any. They tend to compare their work with others, or to an external standard. Information can often be taken as instructions. They will talk about letting other people decide/judge performance, and wanting a checklist or standard to work to. The influencing language you can use to motivate an external person are phrases such as 'X and Y think', 'the experts say', 'others will notice', 'I would strongly recommend' and 'you will get good feedback'.

As a supervisor you may notice the difference between a supervisee who constantly needs feedback and one that sees it as irrelevant. Typically, difficulties can arise when the supervisor works in one way (for example, is internally referenced and gives very little feedback because it is not important for them) and a supervisee who works from the other end of the spectrum (is externally referenced and requires regular and large amounts of feedback to carry out their work). Neither is right or wrong, and having an understanding of this difference can enable you to modify your language and approach to influence the supervisee's behaviour.

Options/procedures

This meta programme looks at how someone approaches their work, and how well they may handle rules.

An *options* person is motivated by opportunities and possibilities to do something in a different way, even if it is working well. They can create a procedure, but are unlikely to follow it. They like choice and prefer development to maintenance activities. They find it difficult to commit, because it may reduce options. They will talk about making choices and expanding choice and possibilities. The influencing language you can use to motivate an *options* person are words like opportunity, choice, alternative, and phrases such as 'here are the options', 'break the rule' and 'there has got to be (another) way'.

A *procedures* person will like to follow a process and be lost without one. They believe there is a right way of doing things, and do not want to break the rules. It is important for them to finish a procedure. They are more interested in how something happened than why. They will talk in stories and about how something happened, and not about choice.

The influencing language you can use to motivate a *procedures* person are phrases like 'the right way' and speak in procedures, such as 'first . . . then . . . after which' and so on.

In supervision, difficulties can arise when each person has a different meta programme. For example, a supervisor who likes looking at options could be frustrated by a supervisee who 'just wants to be told how to do it'. Adapting your style can help the work to be completed.

Specific/general

This meta programme deals with what size or type of information a person prefers to process.

A *specific* person will handle small pieces of information well and like working step by step. They are good at logistics and handling detail. If they are interrupted, they may have to start at the beginning again. They will talk very precisely, using proper nouns and lots of adverbs and adjectives, and use figures and statistics. The influencing language you can use to motivate a *specific* person are words like 'exactly', 'precisely', 'specifically' and details.

A *general* person will prefer to work on an overview or at a conceptual level. They can only concentrate on detail for a short period of time. Because they see the 'big picture', their ideas may be presented in a random order and lack detail. They will talk in simple sentences, use summaries and discuss concepts. The influencing language you can use to motivate a *general* person are words such as 'essentially', 'the main point', 'generally', 'the overall idea', 'summary' and basic concept.

An example of where this might be useful is when a supervisor with a general pattern is frustrated by a supervisee who takes a long time in supervision to explain every detail of a case.

Use of meta programmes

Meta programmes give a structure to explain and appreciate individual differences. Understanding your supervisee's meta programmes can be extremely valuable in building rapport and resolving conflicts or misunderstandings. Knowledge of your own meta programmes is also powerful when working with others, as you become familiar with your own preferences and patterns. Through this awareness you can increase your flexibility and use language to match your supervisee's meta programmes. Your communication will be more effective, which in turn can motivate and influence your team to work at their best.

ACTIVITY **5.2**

Meta programme maps

Think about your team and map out the meta programmes for each member. How do they differ from your own? Does this impact on your relationship?

How can you modify your approach to get the best from each team member?

Unconscious dynamics in supervision

Mirroring/parallel process

This process is useful to consider in a supervision context and can be defined as the unconscious process by which the dynamics of one situation (e.g. the relationship between the service user and the worker) are reproduced in another relationship (e.g. worker and supervisor). For example a worker who is usually well organised becomes quite muddled and distracted when discussing a service user whose chaotic lifestyle they are finding irritating. Similarly the supervisor becomes exasperated at the worker's disorder.

Transference and countertransference

Transference is defined by Brown and Bourne (1996: 90) as 'an unconscious replaying of past dynamics within a current relationship'. The service user can project feelings from previous relationships onto the social worker and treat them as if they were that other person.

Countertransference is the thoughts, feelings and actions taken to counter the feelings being transferred. A supervisee can often be affected by the transference of feelings from the service user (maybe because it triggers associations from their own lives) and react or counter them (Miller, 2012). These unconscious processes are based on the psychodynamic view that past relationships and patterns will become templates for current relationships. It is important that supervision can be a safe place to explore these dynamics.

Hawkins and Shohet (2006) discuss these issues in depth and identify five types of transference:

1. Feelings of the supervisee aroused by the service user

2. Feelings and thoughts of the supervisee provoked by playing the role transferred from the client

3. Feelings, thoughts and actions of supervisee used to counter the transference

4. Projected material from the service user

5. A form of countertransference where the worker wants the service user to change for the worker's sake, rather than for the benefit of the service user.

There are clear links between the discussion about transference and countertransference in the service user/social worker relationship and what goes on in the supervisory relationship. Munro (2011a) states there is evidence of workers treating the service user in the same way as they themselves are treated by their manager. Understanding the power of the unconscious, using self-awareness and reflective skills, is an important aspect of the supervision process. Supervision that pays attention to these issues can open up a very rich seam of information about a service user's unconscious world, as well as the supervisee and supervisor reactions. However, it is important to realise that awareness of parallel process and transference can reveal attitudes and patterns of behaviour outside of the partnership's conscious discussions. These revelations can sometimes be stressful and need to be treated sensitively. The possible effect of mirroring between supervisor and supervisee on the supervisee's practice is further discussed in Chapter 8.

Even if you have reservations about this perspective, it is worth recognising that there may be unvoiced reactions and unexpressed assumptions from the worker and the supervisor which need to be explored. Inquiry reports have often questioned the relationship between social worker and service user, where concerns have been missed, so an awareness of these processes can be important and enable a fuller exploration of practice.

REFLECTION POINT

Consider a recent supervision session and spend some time thinking about what might be some of the unconscious interpersonal dynamics between the participants.

What might be the explanation?

Think about your own past experiences of supervision, particularly when you have found difficulties – how does applying the knowledge of transference or parallel process explain the dynamics?

Interventions in supervision

From the previous discussions, it is clear that the role of supervisor is a highly skilled activity. To enable and empower learning, as well as building productive relationships which keep the needs of the service user at the centre, demands that the supervisor keeps the discussion open and exploratory rather than merely 'advising' or 'instructing'. Within the skills set is an ability to consciously and purposefully use interventions to elicit an achievable outcome. Davys and Beddoe (2010: 131) define these as 'an identifiable piece of verbal and/or non verbal behaviour that is part of the supervisor's service to the supervisee'. They are an essential part of the supervisor's tool kit. Heron (2001) created a six-category intervention analysis for working with service users, and others have been used in counselling which can also be useful for supervision.

Davys and Beddoe (2010) offer a framework of five interventions based on Loganbill *et al.* (1982) which enables supervisors to reflect on what is needed and how that can be provided. It is useful in recognising the variety of approaches that can be taken in a supervision session, as different topics require different skills to reach defined productive outcomes.

1. **Facilitative**: This is the core of supervisory practice where the intention is to provide respect and validation for the supervisee, and an accepting environment to provide safety and privacy. The supervisor will be using skills of whole body listening and paraphrasing to encourage the supervisee to talk about their work. The use of silence creates the space for the practitioner to reflect and decide on their response and is an important and underestimated resource.

2. **Catalytic**: The aim is to promote growth and change through reflection and self-discovery. The supervisor will use open questions to allow the practitioner to explore their practice without direction, to make new connections and understandings for themselves. Reframing is also a useful skill that offers another perspective or lens by which to view the situation, and can help to loosen up rigid thinking. This can be in the form of a question or a statement.

3. **Conceptual**: This intervention is to provide the supervisee with information and knowledge to assist their understanding. This requires the skill of discernment in deciding when and how much information to give. Too much results in dependence and too little will be frustrating and close down discussion. As Davys and Beddoe (2010: 135) observe 'supervision is educative, but it is not formal teaching'. However, Jack and Donnellan (2010) note that newly qualified social workers reported that their supervision often lacked the reference to theories and research that had characterised their student experience. Questions that encourage the practitioner to bring those elements into the discussion will enhance professional practice and does not require the supervisor to 'know it all'.

4. **Confrontative**: This intervention will present the supervisee with issues or aspects of themselves that they have not considered, which are limiting their practice. It will be uncomfortable but, if presented in a respectful, non-adversarial way, it can be a good learning experience. The skill is to formulate a way of challenging the behaviour or attitude within a frame of valuing the practitioner as a person and finding alternatives. Allowing time for the supervisee to talk through and resolve their feelings can result in a positive learning experience.

5. **Prescriptive**: This is used when there are no options and a specific plan of action must be followed. It is usually used in a crisis or to correct a behaviour perceived to be damaging. The skill of being clear and directive whilst maintaining respect is key to being successfully prescriptive. It is probably the least used intervention, as it gives little room for learning or reflection. If it is the main feature of a supervisory relationship then some serious underlying problems need to be addressed.

Use of interventions in a supervisory relationship

Each of these interventions has a use in a supervisory relationship.

Reflect back on your last supervision session and consider which of the five interventions you utilised the most – and the least.

Which one feels more comfortable or least comfortable to use?

What skills do you need to develop further to feel adept in all interventions?

Reflective learning in supervision

Professional judgement is a crucial aspect of a social worker's skill, and critical reflection during supervision will aid this development. Critical reflection according to Fook and Gardner (2007: 21) is the 'unsettling examination of fundamental (socially dominant and often hidden) and individually held assumptions about the social world' to change professional practice. Critical reflection will involve getting in touch with the emotional as well as the cognitive experience.

There are many models and writers that can help you to explore how you can enable critical reflection in your supervisee as well as ensuring you remain critically reflective of your own practice (Gibbs, 1988; Johns and Graham, 1996). First we will consider an adaptation of Kolb's experiential learning cycle (1984) using Carroll's 'knowing model' (2010).

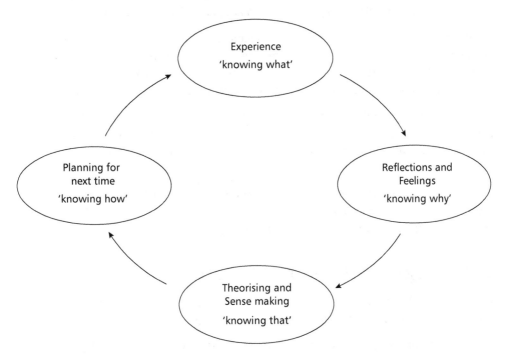

Figure 5.2 Exploring critical reflection

Experience or knowing is being able to recall what we 'do': what skills, abilities, knowledge were used. Reflecting or knowing why is being able to be honest and curious about our actions. The supervisor needs to provide an environment of safety, trust and respect to allow the supervisee to explore openly.

Sense making or knowing that is the knowledge that can emerge from the reflection, and is connected to the theories and frameworks that influence our practice and develops our learning. Planning or knowing how is the translation of sense making into the capability to work differently next time. It is important to emphasise that the essence of this model is that learning is not complete unless the person has taken time to consider all four stages.

Learning styles

Honey and Mumford (1986) developed a model of learning styles that broadly corresponds to the learning cycle:

Activists – they learn by doing. They like to engage in new experiences, enthusiastically and with an open mind. They tend to act first and think later.

Reflectors – they learn by observing and thinking about what happened. They will postpone making definitive conclusions until all perspectives have been explored and can seem very cautious.

Theorists – they like to understand the theory behind the actions and want to make all the information 'fit'. They do not like uncertainty and subjective judgements.

Pragmatists – they like to put the learning into practice, and see little use for abstract ideas. They can be impatient with talking and want to make practical decisions and problem solve.

Questionnaires to determine an individual's predominant style can be found on a number of websites, such as **www.businessballs.com**. There are two possible approaches to learning styles. One is to seek to respond to the supervisee's preferred style; the other is, once a supervisee knows their preferred style, for them to work towards a more balanced style.

There are limitations to this categorising of patterns, not least that can people become rigid about this being 'their way to learn'. However, an exercise with your supervisee to compare learning styles can be a useful and empowering way of talking about preferences in supervision.

Interestingly, Hawkins and Shohet (2006) and Morrison (2007) highlight how people can get 'stuck' in one part of the cycle and this could be a productive way to analyse why someone is not learning and can indicate what might need to happen to move on.

Encouraging critical reflection

There is no quick and simple way to encourage critical reflection. It is a very skilled activity. There are, however, some basic requirements for the supervisor to meet:

1. Creation of an environment that respects the supervisee and allows an honest exploration of practice in a safe space.

2. Ability to listen and allow the time for a supervisee to explore at their pace – without interruptions or advice.

3. Effective questioning. It can be useful to consider what the key questions are that will help the supervisee's exploration, before the session. The aim of the questions is to encourage learning, and therefore should be framed to enable the supervisee to reach their own conclusions. It is not therefore about using questions to arrive at your conclusion!

It is worth noting here that you are in a supervisory relationship that develops over time. This means that you can often spot issues that re-occur across supervision sessions. They might be difficulties or successes. They might constitute a well-practised and proven methodology or suggest that the supervisee is stuck in one approach. You may identify the repetition of a particular emotional response to some cases. There is a danger, in focusing on individual cases and their management, that these longer-term patterns are not identified. Yet they may be very significant and, if fed back to a supervisee, they can offer a valuable insight into their practice. Spotting these longer-term trends demands reflection from you on individual sessions in the context of the longer-term relationship and previous sessions.

ACTIVITY **5.4**

Critical reflection

Consider establishing a bank of questions that you can use in supervision which will encourage critical reflection.

Reflect on a recent supervision session to consider whether the different stages of learning were addressed and how you encouraged critical reflection.

What might you do to improve your approach?

Reflective competence learning model

This model (Taylor, 2007) explains the progression of stages or levels of development in a learning journey. Having awareness of our own development during learning can really help to deepen the experiences and ability to apply the knowledge. It can also be a useful tool in supervision when talking with the supervisee about their stage of development. Gaining an understanding of which stage you or the supervisee have reached can be one way of recording and acknowledging the skills and knowledge that are being developed and applied.

The model is a progression from the more traditional four-stage model that is outlined in the transparent circles (see Figure 5.3). The addition of the fifth stage of reflective competence is the important acknowledgement that learning never stops and experienced practitioners will always be in new and challenging situations. Progression from stage to stage is often accompanied by a feeling of awakening – 'the penny drops' – things 'click' into place for the learner and the person feels like they've made a big step forward; which of course they have.

Key principles of the model

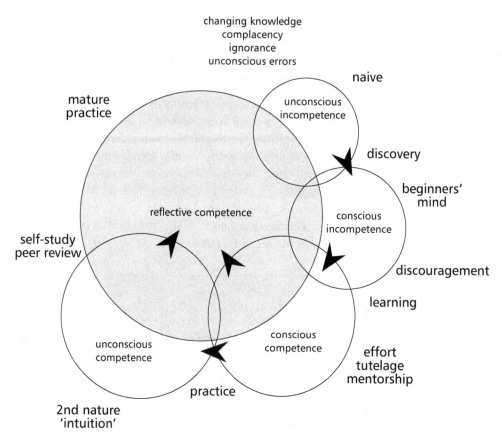

Figure 5.3 Reflective competence learning model (Taylor, 2007. Courtesy of Will Taylor, Chair, Department of Homeopathic Medicine, National College of Natural Medicine, Portland, Oregon, USA, March 2007).

1. Unconscious incompetence

You are not aware of the existence or relevance of the skill area or that you have a particular deficiency in the area concerned. Therefore at this stage you simply do not see the need for learning. Before you can respond to training you have to be aware of the personal benefit you will derive from it.

2. Conscious incompetence

You become aware of the existence and relevance of the skill, and of your own deficiency, and realise that by improvement then your effectiveness will improve. This results in a commitment to practise the new skill. For example, as a new supervisor you may be very uncertain but excited about your role. This may result in a fear of 'what does the supervisee think of me' and a focus on what you are doing. You may be anxious to 'problem solve' and also limit yourself to what you know, rather than being prepared to make decisions and act outside your comfort zone.

3. Conscious competence

Conscious competence is achieved when you can perform a skill reliably, at will, and without assistance. However, you still need to concentrate and think in order to 'get it right' and ideally you need to commit to *practise* to reach the next stage.

4. Unconscious competence

The skill becomes so practised that it enters the unconscious parts of the brain and becomes 'second nature'. After a while of being unconsciously competent you may actually have difficulty in explaining exactly how to do it – the skill has become largely instinctual.

Linking this with supervision might mean that at this stage you will be able to adapt your skills and theories to meet situations, and be more confident in handling the authority of your role. Your confidence has increased but maybe there is a danger of being over-confident, acting unconsciously, and not seeking support when needed.

5. Reflective competence

You challenge your 'unconscious competence', recognising the dangers of complacency, areas of ignorance and unconscious errors. You revisit conscious incompetence, making discoveries about the holes in your knowledge and skills, becoming discouraged, which fuels your motivation to improve. You are continually learning (ongoing conscious competence) and recognise that mature practice encompasses the whole of the model in a constant cycle.

Relating this to supervision, it might sometimes be a challenge to recognise that this stage is important; that there is a constant need to use your critical reflective and analytical skills in the hectic pace of the workplace. In this stage, as a 'mature' supervisor you will be able to balance a trust of your practice wisdom as well as know when to seek support and critical advice. You will be more confident in accepting your authority of the role and working with conflict positively. Your supervisees will notice that you can understand and empathise with their position more readily, rather than being concerned about your own tasks.

REFLECTION POINT

Can you identify with any of the stages of developing reflective competence in your role as an effective supervisor? What one piece of advice or action will you give yourself, to take as another step towards becoming a confident empowering supervisor?

Chapter 6
Working with difficulties in supervision

So far we have looked at how to create and maintain a positive supervisory relationship, but there will always be times when difficulties will arise. This chapter considers some of the important aspects of working through problems.

Feedback

The art or skill of giving and receiving feedback is central to all interventions. Positive or confirmatory feedback, as well as negative or corrective feedback, can be valuable and constructive if delivered and received well. Corrective feedback is probably the most difficult and delivered badly can result in a humiliated and demotivated practitioner. As the basis for learning is often the mistakes we make, however, effective feedback can improve our professional practice. We also think there is a use for 'neutral' feedback where someone feeds back their observations *without any evaluations*. These can result in a rich reflective discussion which develops self-awareness.

As feedback is central to supervision it can be helpful to decide a structure during the contract negotiation process (see Chapter 1). Feedback needs to be heard and so it is important to find the right environment: face-to-face, free from interruption, with time and in private are usually crucial factors.

Giving feedback

Hawkins and Shohet (2006) have created a comprehensive, yet simple framework that brings together the essential principles of giving effective feedback. It is usually referred to by the mnemonic CORBS:

C Clear – Be clear about what feedback you want to give and the outcome you want. Deliver the message confidently and with awareness of how it is being received.

O Owned – The feedback is your perception, and needs to be owned by you. Be clear about what is description and what is your opinion. It is not the absolute truth and therefore use 'I' statements, such as 'I think it is possible that . . .' and 'I'd interpret this as meaning . . .'. And remember feedback can say as much about the giver as the receiver.

R Regular – Feedback is much more meaningful if given regularly. It needs to be included in all supervision sessions and, if about a specific incident, needs to be as close as possible to that time.

B Balanced – A supervisee will gain a more rounded view of their practice if feedback is both corrective and appreciative. It does not need to be forced, so that an equal number of comments are made in one session, but needs to be balanced over time. Drawing attention to positives and achievements as well as identifying problems is, however, important.

S Specific – Most learning is gained from giving as much detail as possible, and generalised statements are open to misinterpretation. Being specific about the practice and the context creates much greater understanding. Refer to the behaviour that can be changed, not personal characteristics that cannot. You may also be specific about what change you would want to see.

Receiving feedback

This is not a passive process and is much more useful if the receiver is actively involved. As a receiver:

- have an open mind, and listen to all the feedback without leaping to judgements or being defensive;

- ask for clarification and evidence;

- consider what you might do differently in the light of the feedback;

- remember it is only information and someone else's perspective and you can choose what you accept;

- remember it is feedback about a behaviour and you are more than just that behaviour in that context;

- say 'thank you'. Receiving feedback is hard but it can be crucial to developing your practice.

REFLECTION POINT

Consider how you use feedback in supervision. What improvements could you make?

How might you encourage supervisees to give you feedback well and how could you help them be good receivers?

Understanding conflict

Conflict in any situation is the struggle between two or more *interdependent* parties who perceive incompatible and opposing needs, goals, wishes, ideas and interests (de Janasz *et al.*, 2011). Conflict occurs when the issues and the need for resolution are perceived to be important.

Conflict is normal and an inevitable part of behaviour. It is based on recognising and valuing the difference and diversity in society. However, our individual view of conflict is often that it is painful and likely to result in negative attitudes and behaviours.

A useful model of understanding conflict, presented by Thomas and Kilman (1976, cited in Huczynski and Buchanan, 2007) identifies five different styles of resolving conflict, which have varying degrees of cooperativeness and assertiveness (see Figure 6.1).

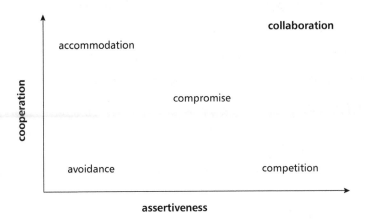

Figure 6.1 Styles of resolving conflict

Individuals often have preferred styles and these have particular disadvantages.

Avoidance: This person ignores conflict and hopes that it will go away. They will withdraw or evade conflict situations, feeling it is harmful. It is an ineffective approach because the situation is likely to remain unresolved and people will be frustrated.

Accommodation: this person is willing to meet the needs of the other at their own expense. They want to keep the peace and be friends with everyone. It can often result in conflict being resolved through submission or compliance, without other views being considered.

Competition: This person uses their power to force their views on others. They often believe that there is only one right answer and hurt feelings are unavoidable. It often results in conflict being resolved at a superficial level, but there is long-term damage to relationships.

Compromise: Often seen as the best way and an agreement that everyone can live with. The person believes that conflict is draining and so wants to reach a quick solution. But sometimes it leaves dissatisfaction on all sides and a better answer could have been achieved with more time.

Collaboration: The person spends time listening to each person to find a way to meet everyone's needs. Conflict resolution is about reaching a good solution, and respecting one another's views. It is not about winning. Even if complete agreement cannot be reached, all parties feel the process has been fair.

Collaboration is often seen as being the 'gold standard' of conflict resolution, and indeed is an outcome to be strived for. However, there are positive aspects to each approach and so the most appropriate style can be dependent on context.

The following section is adapted from research by Thomas, 1977 (cited in Morgan, 2006: 201) and gives examples of where different styles of conflict management are useful.

Avoiding

- When an issue is trivial or more important ones are pressing.
- When you perceive no chance of reaching a satisfactory conclusion.
- When potential disruption outweighs the benefits of resolution.
- To let people cool down and gather perspective.
- When others can resolve more effectively.
- When issues seem tangential or symptomatic of other issues.

Accommodating

- When you find you are wrong – to allow a better position to be heard, to learn, and to show your reasonableness.
- When issues are more important to others than yourself – to satisfy others and maintain cooperation.
- To build social credits for later issues.
- To minimise loss when you are outmatched and losing.
- To allow others to develop by learning from their mistakes.

Competing

- When quick decisive action is vital (e.g. emergencies).
- On important issues where unpopular action needs implementing.
- On important issues with regard to policy and procedures, when you know you are right.

Compromising

- When people with equal power are committed to mutually exclusive goals.
- To achieve temporary settlements to complex issues.
- To arrive at the best possible solutions under time pressure.

Collaborating

- To find an integrative solution when the issues are too important to be compromised.
- When your objective is to learn.
- To merge insights from people with different perspectives.
- To gain commitment by incorporating concerns into consensus.
- To work through feelings which have interfered with a relationship.

ACTIVITY **6.1**

Managing conflict

Consider your approach to management of conflict.

How assertive are you?

How cooperative are you?

Think of situations when you have used different styles and reflect on the outcome.

What would you need to change about your own personal behaviour and attitude to be more collaborative in your approach?

Drama triangle

First created by Stephen Karpman (2007), the Karpman or Drama triangle has become one of the most simple and clear models to use to help to explain unhealthy relationship dynamics. It has its base in the theory of transactional analysis which talks of 'games' being played as people try to find some payoff in a relationship which often involves issues of inequality and power. It is important to remember this describes roles that people take on in relation to others. It does not represent the whole person, and so it is a model for developing self-awareness and understanding, rather than for criticising others' behaviours.

The triangle consists of three roles:

The *victim* who is treated as, or accepts the role of, the victim. In this position the person feels powerless, oppressed and hurt, often because of the behaviours of the persecutor. However, they also abdicate any responsibility for the situation and blame the persecutor for their position. Hence it can be described as bitter-sweet, in that there is a feeling of distress, as well as sometimes a satisfaction in blaming others.

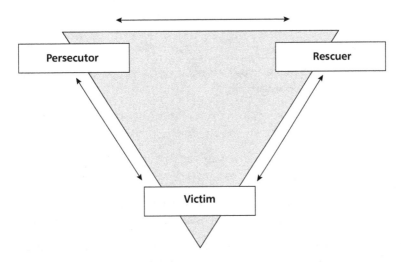

Figure 6.2 Drama triangle for developing self-awareness and understanding

The *persecutor* who pressures, coerces or persecutes the victim. In this position the person is acting only in his own interests and wants to scapegoat and punish the victim for a situation not being as they want it to be, or their failure to meet expectations. They also deny their responsibility for the situation.

The *rescuer* who intervenes to help the situation or the victim. In this position, the person sees the victim as a worthy cause and powerless and so takes over and saves them from the persecutor. The rescuer blames the persecutor for the situation but does not hold any clear boundaries or empower the victim.

The real strength of this model is recognising that all the roles are fluid and interchangeable. It is possible to see how, when one person switches role, the others follow, thus ensuring that the drama is never resolved. For example, the victim can initially be very pleased that the rescuer has arrived, but is then disappointed by their efforts and becomes a persecutor by blaming them for not solving their problems. Or the rescuer becomes unhappy that the victim is not grateful for their intervention and so takes on the role of persecutor. In essence, no one is taking personal responsibility for their attitudes and actions. The phrase 'they made me do it' comes to mind. This avoidance of responsibility is the payoff for the game and, until someone decides to 'step off' the triangle, the problem will continue.

It is also useful to recognise that it does not need three people to make a Drama triangle. The fluidity of the roles means that this can be played out within a dyad, and an analysis of the interactions can show how someone can move through all three roles as the discussion becomes more tense and intractable.

Supervision games

There is clearly a parallel between the roles and games of the Drama triangle, described above, and the games played in supervision that have been identified by Tsui (2005), Kadushin (2002) and Hawthorne (1975).

Below is a list of some of the most common 'games' that can be acted out in supervision and some may be familiar to you. You may be able to see where it fits with the roles of the Drama triangle.

Table 6.1 Games of abdication

They won't let me	Supervisor would like to agree with supervisee, but is blocked by senior management.
Poor me	Supervisor seeks sympathy of supervisee for shortcomings and looks for their support and protection.
I'm really just one of the team	Supervisor sets themselves against organisational practices and policies and seeks to be friends with the supervisee.
So what is your professional opinion?	Supervisor always asks the supervisee what they think and never gives direction or opinions and then agrees with their decision.
I wonder why you really said that	Disagreement by the supervisee is put down to psychological resistance rather than being solved by addressing the issues.

Table 6.2 Games of power

Remember who's the boss	Supervisor uses power of their position to dominate decision making.
I may have to report this	Supervisor threatens to report concerns to senior managers.
Father/mother knows best	Supervisor appears to protect the supervisee whilst dominating supervision.
I'm only trying to help you	The competence of the supervisee is undermined as the supervisor 'rescues' and thereby takes control.

Table 6.3 Supervisee's games

Two against the agency	Supervisee seduces supervisor into ignoring the demands of the organisation.
Mutual admiration society	Supervisee builds a supportive sympathetic relationship that undermines the supervisor's authority.
Treat me don't beat me	Supervisee becomes a casualty that needs help.
Evaluation is not for friends	Supervisee builds a personal friendship that undermines the supervisor's authority.
If you knew the legislation like I know legislation	Supervisee dominates the supervisor with their superior knowledge or personal experience.
I have a little list	Supervisee dominates the agenda or distracts the supervisor onto another topic.
Heading them off at the pass	Supervisee confesses their faults and errors before the supervisor can raise them.
Little old me	Supervisee claims ignorance and limited understanding, forcing the supervisor to take responsibility.
I did what you told me	Supervisee abdicates responsibility for decision-making to the supervisor.
It's all so confusing	Supervisee brings a range of conflicting opinions and perspectives leaving the supervisor to try to reconcile them.

The antidote to games and the Drama triangle

It is easy to see how 'stuck' a relationship can get on the Drama triangle. Although we may feel dissatisfied with the interactions, we find it difficult to find an alternative. Self-awareness and a willingness to change are first steps, and some of the principles around conflict management will help (see later in this chapter). What is incontrovertible is that the games are impossible to play with only one player. So in essence, a change in one person's behaviour can break the cycle.

An alternative model called the Winner's triangle (Choy, 1990, cited in Burgess, 2005) offers a framework to free up the dynamics of disempowerment in the Drama triangle. Its strength is in helping everyone to take the appropriate responsibility and become 'response-able' (Burgess, 2005: 98). It offers an analysis and strategies to overcome the abdication of responsibility that the Drama triangle analysis has revealed. The three positions correspond, but are very different to those in the Drama triangle.

The persecutor is replaced by an *assertive* position. The person is acting in their own interests, but is taking responsibility for what they want and asking for it rather than punishing others for not getting it. So the angry blaming persecutor becomes assertive and able to make clear requests, whilst acknowledging another's position.

The rescuer is replaced by a *caring* position. In this position the person remains in touch with their own needs and no longer tries to solve the problems of others. They are aware of how the other person is responsible for themselves and will maintain appropriate boundaries that can be motivating and empowering, rather than taking over and disempowering the other.

The victim is replaced by a *vulnerable* position. This can be a powerless and unpleasant position and somewhere that we prefer to avoid. The motivation to sidestep such feelings can result in taking on the roles of the Drama triangle. The challenge, as Burgess (2005: 104) says, is daring to be vulnerable. By being vulnerable the person accepts responsibility for his/herself, and becomes aware of their needs. In some ways this can be empowering, as it can allow problems to be approached from another perspective. Acknowledging the reality of being hurt and vulnerable means they are no longer a victim and therefore not open to the manipulations of a persecutor or rescuer.

A change of behaviour in any of the positions can lead to the opening of options and creative dialogue, and the person may need the courage to cope with the other(s) not changing immediately and maintaining their new role.

Burgess concludes that the Drama and Winner's triangles are useful tools to understand the dynamics of relationships and, when used collaboratively, give a common language to use to change damaging patterns of behaviour. It is also a way of building our emotional intelligence.

However, it is worth bearing in mind that one of the purposes of games is to mitigate the negative influences of organisational power and ease the potential tension between supervisor and supervisee. Games are therefore almost a given, a necessary part of the supervisory relationship. They do not necessarily get in the way of decision-making or detract from the relationship. It is always a matter of degree, with the supervisor having to judge whether a behaviour has become destructive or unhelpful.

ACTIVITY **6.2**

Games and supervision

Consider a current situation where you have some concern about a supervisory relationship.

Can you identify any games that you are playing?

What might be the games being played by your supervisees?

Are the games having negative effects on your supervision?

Using the Winner's triangle – what might be some questions or statements that you can make to break the cycle?

Difficult conversations

As a supervisor, there will be many occasions where you will need to have a difficult conversation or to challenge someone. Although we have recognised that conflict is normal, many of us do not communicate well in these situations. Rosenberg's model of non-violent communication (2003) can be really helpful when considering how to manage a potentially difficult situation. He suggests there are four steps to communicating well when there is disagreement:

1. Be clear about what happened – observation without evaluation.

2. Connect with and express feelings (not thoughts).

3. Connect with and express needs.

4. Work out what would help to resolve the situation and make a request.

1. **What happened?**

It can be quite difficult to make non-judgemental statements, but this is an important first step to understanding the outside stimulus that triggers the conflict feeling and then communicating what has happened. Rosenberg talks of 'Observing without Evaluation'. This involves being specific about time and context, referring to behaviours and not the person.

For example, you might want to say: *'Sam – you are always late for duty and letting the team down.'* This becomes: *'Sam – you have been an hour late for duty three times in the last two weeks. Other members of the team have changed appointments to cover for you.'*

2. What are my feelings?

Distinguish between feelings and thoughts. Underlying the thoughts are the feelings that are driving the behaviours. Thoughts also can have hidden judgements attached. Learn to know the difference between the words that describe feelings and those that describe thoughts.

Tip: If you are not sure whether it is a feeling or thought that you are describing, ask the question *'How does that make me (you) feel?'*

For example: *'I feel he is not pulling his weight?'* (a thought)

Question: *'So how does that make you feel?'*

Answer: *'That it is not fair on those who have to cover him.'* (another thought)

Question: *'So how does that make you feel?'*

Answer: *'I feel disappointed and upset.'* (a feeling)

The example so far: *'I feel disappointed and upset when you have been an hour late for duty three times in the last two weeks . . .'*

This is an important distinction and helps to be able to understand the emotions that underlie conflict. Thoughts do not create emotions on their own – only when they are attached to feelings. It is also important to remember that our feelings are our responsibility and come from our own internal processing of events: someone's behaviour may be the stimulus – but it is not the cause.

3. What are my needs?

Rosenberg states that at the root of a dispute is an unmet need and the negative feelings are caused by that unmet need. The unmet need should be owned by the person, and is not the responsibility of the other party. This is the key to this model and is the way that can unlock the defensive and stuck positions. It means that the parties start to focus on what is underlying the emotions from a problem-solving place, rather than a blame place.

For example: *'I feel disappointed when you have been an hour late for duty three times in the last two weeks BECAUSE I need to feel confident that the duty rota will run smoothly to meet the expectations of the agency.'*

4. What do I want to happen – as a request?

Work out what it is that you would like, based on your unmet need – and remember it is a request, a suggestion to solve the problem and not a demand. Make the request clear and specific, and make it as a positive statement (i.e. what you want, not what you don't want). This will mean the request is made with respect for both parties.

The final statement in the example would then be:

'I feel disappointed when you have been an hour late for duty three times in the last two weeks because I need to feel confident that the duty rota will run smoothly to meet the expectations of the agency. Would you please be on time, or make sure that you have arranged a duty swop that is written on the rota.'

This then opens out the conversation for a constructive dialogue about future behaviour.

You also need to know about the other person, and the four steps are used to find this out.

Before asking the questions it is helpful to hold these two assumptions:

- that their behaviour is the best it can be in the current context;
- underneath their behaviour is a feeling and an unmet need.

The questions are asked from a position of respect and empathy and genuine curiosity.

1. What do you know about the situation: what did you observe?
2. What are your feelings?
3. What do you need?
4. What do you want me to do/say . . .?

Next steps: managing the conversation

1. Prepare yourself and know that you are able to be curious and respectful about the other person. If not, then leave it until you are.
2. Develop and maintain rapport with the person.
3. Summarise your needs and requests.
4. Ask the four step questions.
5. Listen well and if when you say something they cannot hear – listen more.

It is important that they are able to express all their feelings and needs – it can take time.

6. Both now consider the requests and needs – is there any common ground?

    Yes – nearly there – go to step 7.

    If not then:

    - empathise with their position – keep compassionate with self and other;
    - ask what is important about those needs and requests – search for the common ground.

    Still not there?

    Ask yourself: Are you really willing to solve the dispute – What do you gain by not resolving it? What more can *you* do to find a resolution? And if there is still no resolution, agree to disagree and decide the next step on that basis.

7. Create a collaborative solution.
8. Decide on the next specific step.

Tips for managing the conversation

Be compassionate and respectful of your needs. If it is difficult: stop – breathe – recognise your needs in the moment.

Consider using an anchor (see pages 60–1) to maintain your emotional and cognitive state.

Working with a supervisee on a performance problem

Perhaps the biggest challenge for a supervisor is to effectively manage a performance problem. This scenario is necessarily difficult for both supervisor and supervisee and one where the legitimate power of the supervisor becomes most apparent. It can be distressing for both supervisor and supervisee, so managing the emotion and the relationship is as significant as managing the task.

Following the strategies outlined above will help to manage the relationship and provide a basis for finding a way forward.

In addition, you will need to be honest and transparent about the policies, procedures and your responsibilities and power within the context of the organisation. Adapting guidelines by Yukl (2006), we have developed the following recommendations for good practice in managing a performance problem:

- **Gather information about the performance problem.** Gather information that is evidence-based and specific. Think back over supervision sessions. You may also need to check records and talk to others. Understanding the problem also demands exploration with the supervisee.

- **Fair and transparent judgements**. It is important that you can be seen to be fair and have reflected carefully on the evidence. It is also worth considering to what extent the problem is 'theirs' and can be rectified by them. Your preferences and practices may also be significant: are you imposing the way you would do things on the supervisee?

- **Feedback.** Use elements of CORBS (page 81) to ensure that this is effective.

- **Explain the adverse impact of ineffective behaviour.** This makes the process meaningful. Remember that it can also have a negative impact on the supervisee, as well as people who use services, so ask about this as well. Supervisees can sometimes be well aware of the problem.

- **Mutually identify the reasons for inadequate performance.** This is the crucial goal, mutuality. If you can come to a shared agreement of the problem and then objectively explore possible causes together, there is a strong possibility that you will together bring an improvement.

- **Ask the person to suggest remedies.** This is another essential strategy and helps them to own the solutions. You may need to help them though. They are also often not alone in experiencing problems: encourage them to explore with colleagues how they handle this aspect of practice. Bear in mind that the supervisee can be stuck, and there can be a payoff for the way they currently do things and negative effects of change.

- **Express confidence in the person.** You need to have and hold a positive view of the people you supervise, including their ability to develop and improve their practice and their essential professional integrity and desire to do so. You need to be genuine in your desire to help find good solutions.

- **Reach agreement on specific action steps.** If the engagement and ownership of the staff member is crucial, you also need to be specific about what will be done and when it will be done: both the relationship and the task need equal attention.

- **Summarise the discussion and verify agreement.** This can be a very emotional process for both of you, so a summary is essential to ensure mutual understanding and this should be recorded and agreed. Recognise how hard it has been and your shared achievement in addressing it together.

ACTIVITY **6.3**

The challenge of performance management in supervision (part 1)

Whilst supervision can be very rewarding it can also be very difficult and stressful. Sometimes you may not be successful: some problems experienced by supervisees can be long standing, resulting from experiences in the past, and you can inherit problems that should have been addressed earlier. Look at the fictionalised scenarios below.

What do you think was happening in the supervisory relationship to explain the comments from supervisors?

1. Working with M has been a nightmare for me. The rest of the team are easy to supervise but she brings and gives nothing and has the most problematic practice as well. I have tried just about everything. If I challenge her she just gets hissy and ignores me. She thinks she knows best, but although she was probably once a very good practitioner, she's out of date. I worry about it over the weekend, I even dream about her. It would help if I could share it with my supervisor but she's on the sick, has been for months.

2. It's over a year now I've been trying to get him on board. I'd pretty much given up. Then suddenly he just said that he wasn't really coping and hadn't been for some time. We were able to talk it through properly. He said he'd thought about leaving social work but he's making improvements now. Last supervision he said how much happier he was. What helped? Sheer bloody persistence, you can't believe how much energy it has taken. Kindly persistence? Well maybe.

3. I'm so proud of this but it took every bit of professional skill I've got. I fouled up at the start and put her nose out of joint by challenging her rather clumsily. Truth is we both felt bad and found it difficult, with her not getting the job and me being younger. I was so angry with her, she was so rude, you cannot believe. I thought about it a bit though and started to see her side of it. Some of it was us getting off on the wrong foot, but it must have been getting to her, she must have worried about what might happen with no records being kept for so many cases, and she'd just not turn up for meetings or even for supervision. Anyway I stuck with it, we had to deal with it, but I guess I started to see it through her eyes and she eventually saw where I was coming from.

4. The result of all that was that she left, just resigned. She came to see me, though, to say how much better she was, that social work wasn't really for her. I'd like to think she moved on to better things but, well you don't really know, do you?

ACTIVITY **6.3** *(CONT.)*

5. It was a near run thing. He was so disorganised it wasn't true. We kept agreeing actions and he just didn't do anything. Then he just smiled weakly at me when I pointed it out. I had decided I would have to lay down the law when I realised I was starting to sound like my father. So instead I said it was up to him. I went carefully through the options and the consequences and let him decide. He had been almost inviting me to bully him; as soon as I gave him the choice, including getting disciplined, perhaps even dismissed, he was fine. We worked well together after that.

ACTIVITY **6.4**

The challenge of performance management in supervision (part 2)

Now review the team you supervise. Identify those supervisory relationships where you are managing a performance problem. Which ones do you think you are making progress with and why? Which ones are stuck? Why might this be? What could you try differently? What impact is managing problem performance having on you?

Section 3
The organisational context

There is a danger of focusing too much on supervision practice without recognising the importance of the broader organisational context in which it is set. This context can have considerable impact on the quality of supervision and its outcomes in several ways:

- Organisational and team culture – the culture of the organisation and team in which supervision is being carried out will have an impact on supervision practice (Hawkins and Shohet, 2006). A learning culture will support it whilst, for instance, a blame culture can undermine it.

- Current initiatives to improve supervisory practice, in order to be successful, may depend on changes in organisational culture, which demand organisation-wide change supported by an organisation-wide approach.

- Other organisational systems processes and activities interact with supervision and can influence its quality – for instance, how training and development and performance are managed will influence supervision. Also, social work practice is not just dependent on supervision, and supervisors need to mediate or interface with the wider organisation and environment to be effective.

- Different organisational levels will influence supervision and need to be coordinated to bring improvements and maintain its quality – for instance, the supervision which supervisors receive from middle managers will either support or undermine their practice.

Some of these dimensions may be hard for you as a supervisor to influence, whilst others are more in your control. Crucially, whilst one could argue that individual supervision is the most important activity in ensuring service quality, attention needs to be given to this wider context, because of the positive or negative influence it can have on practice and therefore ultimately the service.

Chapter 7
Developing a learning culture

Learning organisations

The impact of the broader organisational culture on learning and development and the quality of services or products has been recognised for some time in the private sector and has been expressed as the theory of learning organisations. Senge (1990), for instance, outlined the key features of a learning organisation as:

Systems thinking – seeing organisations as networks of people which interact together to deliver a service. Good services and service problems are generated by the network and the interaction. Individuals should not be blamed for problems, and solutions lie with improving systems.

Personal mastery – accepting the importance of systems, individuals still need to dedicate themselves to developing their own skills and expertise so that they can contribute to the organisation.

Overcoming mental models – not getting stuck in standard responses and solutions and searching for innovative ways of working.

Shared vision and values – people must be freed up to play a part in a learning organisation and should not be micro-managed. A strong shared vision and shared values ensures a common direction and allows people to work independently to agreed ends.

Team working and learning – the secret to providing quality services and improving them is working and learning together. Teams generate energy and, by combining expertise, generate innovative approaches.

Senge's work became an international best seller because it claimed that developing the features of a learning organisation would give companies a competitive edge. In health and social care, this same idea was expressed by Hawkins and Shohet (2006) when they suggested that a learning or development culture is necessary if supervision is to flourish. More recently, attention has been given to developing learning organisations in both health and social care, as a learning culture is seen as countering a controlling approach and too much of a focus on performance management (Munro, 2011b).

However, some writers have argued that the dominant organisational culture in health and social care, as it is hierarchical and top-down, means that learning organisations are unlikely to succeed (Gould and Baldwin, 2004). Policy makers are more optimistic; for instance Munro

(2011b) recently made this a key feature of the Social Work Reform Board agenda and SCIE (2004) has developed an audit tool to help organisations develop the features of a learning organisation. The proposal is that teams at different levels of an organisation should audit their practice and plan for improvement. We have included the audit tool in the appendices. Take a look at it, as it can readily be seen how broader structures, systems and behaviours could make a difference to your supervision. You could use the audit tool to explore whether your organisational culture is that of a learning organisation and to plan for improvement.

When we have used this method with team leaders and managers, they have often pointed out that there is a difference between their organisation and team culture, with their team culture being closer to a learning organisation than their wider organisation. This opens up the possibility of creating a 'micro-culture' in a team which would try to achieve the features of a learning organisation. This could cause tension and some conflict with the wider organisation, but it could also have a very positive effect on supervision. A community of practice approach could therefore be a valuable way forward for a first line supervisor.

Wenger (1998, 2006) is one of the proponents of communities of practice. He suggests that communities of practice are:

> *groups of people who share a concern or a passion for something they do and learn how to do it better as they interact regularly.*

He argues that learning and development are social activities and dependent on the community in which the individual practices. This means:

> *Members of a community of practice are practitioners. They develop a shared repertoire of resources: experiences, stories, tools, ways of addressing recurring problems – in short a shared practice.*

> *Communities of practice enable practitioners to take collective responsibility for managing the knowledge they need, recognising that, given the proper structure, they are in the best position to do this.*

(Wenger, 1998)

What is interesting is the suggestion that a community of practice can work independently of the wider organisation to ameliorate its impact. Wenger (1998) gives an example of new software which is introduced from the top in an organisation and is quickly found by workers to be ineffective and to disadvantage vulnerable customers. When workers protest, they are ignored and told to get on with using the new software, but the community of practice, independently of the organisation and the management structure, find ways to make it work and so protect the customer. A community of practice therefore works independently of the organisation in solving organisational problems. We observed that this separateness was expressed by the line managers and supervisors we worked with, who saw their teams as more of a learning organisation than the wider organisation in which they function.

Another important aspect of a community of practice is ameliorating the unpleasantness of organisational life by socialising it. The community almost provides a family life within the organisation, celebrating birthdays and other events, supporting individuals in difficulties and allowing a place for the personal in organisational life in the friendly interaction between colleagues. Many jobs in health and social care by their nature are very stressful. A positive supportive community of practice can do much to make this bearable and can allow the expression of some of the negative experiences to which we are subject.

We hold the perspective that developing a community of practice is a very viable approach to learning and development and the management of practice and offers a useful strategy for line managers and team leaders in health and social care (Gray *et al.*, 2010b). Its strengths are:

- many health and social care leaders and managers have a team orientation and they can be skilled groupworkers;

- it will be easier in a wider organisation that is a learning organisation, but otherwise it still offers a way forward that is in the control of the team leader and the team: it provides a strategy for team leadership and team development;

- it accords with our professional value base: it values individuals but recognises their social nature as well and expresses a faith in the ability of human beings to grow and develop;

- individual supervision can be seen to support and be supported by a community of practice;

- professionals can be readily mobilised to contribute to and support the team and it is recognised as essential to professional capability that they do so.

Crucially, it also does justice to the lived experience of being a health or social care practitioner. No one has ever carried out this audit, but if you tracked one of your supervisees through a typical week, their formal and informal contact with you is only a small part of their experience. The rest of the time they are interacting with the wider team and people outside it, and all of these interactions are potentially ones in which the individual learns and develops their practice and problem solves.

CASE STUDY 7.1

My first supervisor was really good, but my next team leader, although he was a nice bloke, was only really any good at knowing the right procedures. The team was great though, they would always offer me advice and guidance and there were senior practitioners in other teams as well who were really helpful. I also often went to a training manager who was based in the office, she really knew her stuff and we used to spark each other off. So having an iffy supervisor didn't stop me improving my practice. In fact, if you ask me, it wasn't my degree or the supervision that developed me as a social worker, it was that team.

Developing a learning culture as the basis for a community of practice

A key question is how do we set about building a positive and supportive community of practice? A situational leadership approach would seem ideal, initially being more directive but then working at developing independent practitioners and a participative team culture. Another very valuable leadership theory which, alongside situational leadership, can offer a useful way forward in developing a community of practice is distributed leadership, which we discussed from page 41 onwards.

Apart from a situational and distributed leadership approach which encourages participation, how else might one set about developing a community of practice? The key lies in reverting back to Hawkins and Shohet's point about the importance of a learning culture to support supervision. We asked what a learning culture looks like in health and social care, and decided that there wasn't one but four possible learning cultures (Gray *et al.*, 2008):

- a professional learning culture;
- a managed learning culture;
- a humanistic learning culture;
- a democratic learning culture.

Social work perhaps needs a diverse learning culture that embraces the features of all four cultures, as detailed in Table 7.1.

Comparison of learning and development cultures

Table 7.1 Social work learning cultures

PROFESSIONAL LEARNING CULTURE (as strived for by professional bodies)	MANAGED LEARNING CULTURE (as strived for by human resource management)
Professional college sets practice standards and practitioners have a long-term relationship with their college.	Practice standards are quality standards determined by managers.
Professionals manage their own learning and development.	Learning and development is the responsibility of line managers.
Competence determined by experienced professionals using personal judgement.	Competence determined by appraisal or assessment against published standards.
Learning and development driven by personal career and practice agendas. Strong emphasis on professional value base.	Learning and development driven by business need and business case. Strong emphasis on cost effectiveness.
Learning and development evaluated in terms of professional growth and development.	Learning and development evaluated according to business outcomes and impact on the service.
Supervision is focused on personal development.	Supervision is focused on case and service management.

Table 7.1 Continued

Sanctions are removal of professional accreditation and judgement is made by peers.	Sanctions are managerial, i.e. progression, reward or use of capability procedures.
Dialogue with a fellow professional, critical reflection and professional education are crucial vehicles for personal development.	A range of training and development methods are used according to learning need and cost efficiency considerations.
Professionals are expected to contribute to professional development as a duty.	Professional trainers and consultants are employed, relationships are commercial.
HUMANISTIC LEARNING CULTURE (as strived for by therapeutic communities)	**DEMOCRATIC LEARNING CULTURE (as strived for by total quality management)**
Individuals are liberated by reflecting on their actions and the consequences of their actions for others and making choices. The community both challenges behaviour and supports individuals.	Organisational and social expertise and creativity can be increased if the power relations which exclude some from problem solving and decision-making are addressed.
Learning and development are natural human activities. Group influence and experiences can be mobilised to bring personal change.	Learning and development are natural human activities but power relationships in society seek to use them to control.
Competence is competence in life and is about self-actualisation.	If groups are liberated they can make a contribution to social competence, that is, to the capability of society or an organisation to learn and develop.
Learning and development is driven by social and personal needs which are inseparable.	Learning and development should be directed towards the social good.
Learning and development is evaluated in terms of personal growth and development and social responsibility.	Learning and development is evaluated in terms of the contribution it makes to social outcomes.
Supervision focuses on personal life experience and emotional responses to situations.	Supervision is by peers through group problem solving and decision-making. The focus is on group working experiences and social or organisational outcomes.
Dialogue and reflection are crucial activities facilitated by a counsellor or mentor or by friends and colleagues.	Group discussion and analysis are crucial activities facilitated by peers.
Engagement in learning and development must be a matter of personal choice.	Engagement in learning and development is a social duty but voluntarism is espoused.

(Gray et al., 2008)

So the learning culture of a community of practice in health and social care perhaps needs to be a 'superordinate' one (Gray *et al.*, 2008), i.e. one which embraces all four learning cultures and integrates them – for each has an important part to play. It is important that individuals are active in managing their own CPD; training audit and training provision makes a crucial contribution to learning and development as does performance management and appraisal. Yet alongside these perhaps more managed cultures, there is a need for the more communal humanistic and democratic learning cultures which support an emotionally supportive team environment and a team of active problem solvers seeking to improve practice and the service.

This gives an agenda for the team leader wanting to develop a community of practice. They need to work on all four team cultures in a coordinated approach. Reaching for a participative leadership style will be essential in all of the activities (see Table 7.2).

Table 7.2 Engaging the team

Engage the team in developing and improving continuing professional development and critical reflective practice including developing individual supervision.	Engage the team in managing training, performance management and appraisal.
Engage the team in developing an emotionally supportive team environment.	Engage the team in joint problem solving.

In the sections below, we will explore the dimensions that need attention in developing a community of practice. Bear in mind as we explore these dimensions that your leadership, as discussed above, is essential throughout, as only a participative and developmental/ empowering approach will support a community of practice. Each culture then supports and enhances the others. Developing critical reflective practice is addressed in Chapter 5, and is also an essential part of leading and developing CPD.

Continuing professional development (CPD)

With responsibility for the registration of social workers passed to the Health and Care Professionals Council, now is a good time to explore how effective your team's current practice is and plan for improvement using its standards (HCPC, 2012). Some interesting features of its approach are:

- it doesn't require a set number of days' or hours' activity; rather, it is left to the individual's discretion;

- you are expected to make use of a range of CPD activities listed;

- you are expected to ensure that your CPD has improved your practice and enhanced service delivery. This involves exploring the impact of your CPD on people who use services;

- you must keep a record of your CPD activity and, if you are chosen to be audited, you will be asked to produce this as part of a profile that also includes evidence. It lists the sort of evidence you may wish to include.

It is worth noting that:

> If a registrant provides false or misleading information in their CPD profile, we would deal with them under our fitness to practise procedures. This could lead to them being struck off the Register so that they can no longer practise. Someone who is struck off our Register cannot apply to be registered again for five years.
>
> (HCPC, 2012: 4)

So they would seem to offer a flexible approach with considerable discretion but a rigorous approach to auditing that means that individuals must keep an updated record of activity and also at least identify possible evidence as it is generated or, perhaps more usefully, collect it as it is generated.

You can find the HCPC's standards at **www.hcpc-uk.org**, together with their examples of CPD activities and examples of evidence. It is a good idea to keep an eye on this website so that you are up to speed as new documents are added to offer direct guidance to social workers.

This change in approach offers the opportunity for you to review current practices with your team and plan for improvement, and it perhaps demands a more thoughtful approach to CPD than in the past. Whilst team discussion on current practices and the new standards from the HCPC will be valuable, supervision can play an important role in supporting good practice. It is a pity that supervision is not given more prominence by the HCPC as a crucial CPD activity. However, many of their categories are covered by supervision, such as learning by doing, reflective practice, coaching, discussion, peer review, gaining and learning from experience. Supervision can readily be seen, therefore, as a crucial CPD activity and a valuable source of evidence.

ACTIVITY 7.1

Developing a CPD improvement plan

Review the HCPC's standards, their examples of CPD activities and their examples of evidence by going to their website. How does your team's practices compare with their standards? Consider the menu below and develop with your team a CPD improvement plan which will achieve them, including:

- *Agreeing and reviewing a personal development plan.*
- *Evaluating together the impact of CPD on the supervisee's practice.*
- *Evaluating together the impact on the service and the benefit to the service user.*

Managing training

Managing training is a crucial activity which directly supports and is supported by supervision. Supervision allows for training needs to be identified and fed, as a training audit, to a training section to inform commissioning, and it also allows the impact of the training on practice to be facilitated and evaluated. Any difficulties individuals might be having in applying learning to practice can also be identified and worked on in supervision.

Accepting that other forms of personal development, including supervision, may have a bigger impact on practice, formal training has a very important contribution to make, which means that its management deserves attention. Some of its advantages are:

- some learning needs are best met by an organisational expert outside of the team, e.g. IT training, health and safety;

- it allows expert knowledge to be brought in from outside the organisation. This can be particularly important for new developments and legislation;

- it allows a wide audience to be addressed, so new national policies and new organisational strategies and local initiatives can be supported;

- time away from the workplace can be a valuable opportunity to reflect and learn;

- it offers opportunity to learn alongside peers from other teams, and group discussion and interaction can do much to increase understanding and application;

- provision of a 'core' of training can do much to assist with induction and prepare people for practice, i.e. formal training gives structure to personal development;

- if it's accredited, it can encourage people to progress and achieve qualifications which can be motivational.

What are the other dimensions of the effective management of training? Taking post-qualifying training as an example, research has identified a range of problems which can be seen as applying to the management of most training provision (Brown *et al.*, 2005). We have identified them in Table 7.3 alongside the role you can play in rectifying them, which readily illustrates the importance of supervision in making training effective.

Table 7.3 Tackling problems in training provision

Poor completion rates, unclear and unequal nomination processes. Problems with release and lack of time.	Ensuring all your supervisees have access to training is crucial and you need to manage their workload alongside the rest of the teams to ensure they can be released and their work covered. They will benefit from additional study time as well (not easy but it does make a difference).
Lack of knowledge and understanding in the organisation of provision.	You and your team need to know what is available. Your supervisees can help with this, i.e. exploring resources available, but supervision is a crucial forum for informing and briefing people.
Lack of time to reflect and lack of study skills including reflection on practice.	Supervision offers a valuable opportunity to develop reflective skills and reflect on application of training to practice situations.

Table 7.3 Continued

Lack of support from line managers and commitment from the organisation. Experiences not being integrated into supervision, personal development planning and CPD before, during and after the programme.	It helps if there is an organisational-wide commitment to training and development but your attitude and support are crucial – in many respects you are the organisation, and you link training, through supervision, to CPD planning and practice.
Not being able to bring new practices back to the team and implement them.	You can do much to facilitate this in supervision and can encourage supervisees to share training with the team.
Lack of monitoring and evaluation.	Supervision offers the best opportunity to determine if training has been carried into practice and therefore gauge its effectiveness. You need to feed back to the training team the views of you and your supervisees.
Lack of IT skills, access to IT, study skills and unrecognised learning needs, e.g. dyslexia.	Supervision allows you opportunity to assist individuals with particular learning needs and other difficulties where otherwise they will be unsupported. Individual barriers to learning are also barriers to practice.
Lack of support and follow up if candidates are not successful.	Supervisees can struggle to learn and to apply learning to practice. As a supervisor at the interface with practice and with a close working relationship with them, you can do much to assist with this.

(Developed from Brown et al., 2005: 75–80)

REFLECTION POINT

Reviewing the management of training in your team with reference to the table above, what could you do to improve the management of training?

Individual performance management or appraisal

Individual performance management or appraisal plays an important part in managing training and development, and supervision is essential to its effectiveness. It is a formal system for regularly reviewing an individual's performance and making judgements about their level of attainment. It is often an annual event, sometimes with reviews, and it usually results in the production of a report. A key outcome of an appraisal is usually objectives for improving performance and it is also often used to plan personal development. Rarely, it can also encompass career planning.

In the private sector it can be linked to reward systems such as performance related pay, and, although this is unusual in health and social care, it is sometimes the basis for determining whether or not someone is awarded an increment and can influence promotion.

The individual performance management process appears to be a relatively simple one and it is a problem-solving, iterative process.

However, this simplicity masks a complexity which quickly generates problems in practice. For instance, data collection is often neglected or lacking in method. At best, organisations use 360-degree feedback (Armstrong, 2006), but at worse the effectiveness of the whole process is dependent on a manager's often prejudiced perceptions. In contrast, in health and social care, regular supervision should mean that a supervising manager often has a very rich picture of an individual's practice.

Analysis of performance is dependent on the quality of the data collected and the quality of the analysis. A range of comparators and points of reference are commonly used in organisations to help managers in making judgements:

- competencies or standards of performance;
- organisational strategy or objectives;
- individually agreed objectives;
- delegated projects;

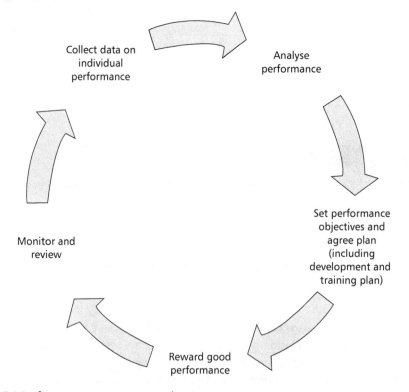

Figure 7.1 Performance management cycle

- rating system linked to performance pay levels;

- organisational performance measures;

- job specification.

In health and social care, codes of practice and professional values offer other points of reference and you may find you draw on a range of comparators. The new Professional Capabilities Framework (PCF) will provide another point of reference. Judging performance is complex because practice is complex. In fact it could be argued that evaluating performance is the most demanding of professional activities. Competencies and the new capability framework can help, but in reality practice cannot be that clearly defined.

Problems with individual performance management have been identified for at least half a century, perhaps with little success for most organisations in overcoming them. There is evidence that the weakest part of an individual performance management system is the familiar attempt to balance a focus on individual performance with improving organisational systems. For instance, the section in documentation that seeks to identify how the organisation might better support an individual and their performance is typically completed badly or not at all, indicating that opportunity is not taken to explore what the organisation can do to better support someone's practice (Mullins, 2007).

It is usual to stress the importance of appraisal not just being a one-off event and point to the need for managers to manage performance on an everyday basis (Armstrong, 2006; Mullins, 2007). This is often accompanied by the idea that there should be 'no surprises' in an appraisal event, performance issues having been identified and responded to throughout the year. This exhortation is worth examining because it perhaps points to the weaknesses of individual performance management:

- if you create a formal event and often monitor its completion as an organisational performance measure, don't be surprised if it takes over from everyday practice;

- stressing the importance of everyday performance management is one thing, but writers often significantly fail to offer guidance on how this might be managed. This inevitably means that the formal 'one-off' event dominates.

Health and social care, therefore, has a great advantage over the private sector – its established tradition of providing regular management supervision. Supervision offers the opportunity to get performance management right, as it provides a regular opportunity for a manager and a professional to explore performance together throughout the year, responding to problems and planning for improvement.

One could argue that regular supervision therefore makes an annual appraisal irrelevant, but there are a number of good reasons for seeing it as enhancing supervision. It allows opportunity for supervisors and supervisees to step out of the intensity of everyday supervision and consider overall performance. It also allows trends and themes to be identified which individual sessions might miss.

As a professional it can be argued that you have the right to appraisal. Appraisal means judgements about overall performance and therefore reward and promotion are fair, which means open and transparent. It provides opportunity for positive feedback and for a supervisee to take credit for achievements across the year. It allows the chance for job satisfaction to be reviewed as well as achievement and the psychological contract to be addressed. That is to say, a supervisor can take the opportunity to identify issues which are undermining the quality of a supervisee's working experience and respond. Appraisal can therefore have a big impact on staff retention and wellbeing. Career planning is also an opportunity not to be missed, and it is crucial to your supervisee's long-term motivation and engagement and the future of the organisation and service. So, taking time to look at career ambitions, and how these can be supported and achieved, is a valuable investment.

Appraisal also offers the opportunity to review the effectiveness of supervision together, and objectives for improving supervision for both supervisor and supervisee could be valuable outcomes from an appraisal.

Centrally imposed and often crude performance measures have meant that performance management has been seen to undermine supervision (Munro, 2011a). But this does not mean that good performance management cannot be at the heart of supervision, and we must not allow the current reaction to a period of over-control to distract us from good practice in performance management. Maintaining and developing the quality of practice is essential to the service and the wellbeing of people who use services, and this demands making judgements about performance.

What are the challenges to making appraisals positive for your team?

Individual performance management and appraisal has long been noted as being hateful to staff and managers (McGregor, 1957). Crucially, rather than being seen as essential, a right or an opportunity, it is often viewed negatively. Most of the problems associated with individual performance management can be seen to stem from its nature as perhaps the point where the exercise of organisational power is made most obvious for individual staff members and has most impact on them. This is particularly the case when it is linked to pay or progression (Armstrong, 2006). Very early on, McGregor (1957) associated it with his controlling 'Theory X' management style and, apart from its negative impact on staff motivation, also noted that managers do not like standing in judgement over others.

McGregor suggests a shift away from the concept of appraisal – something that is done to you – to 'analysis', with the individual taking responsibility and control of the process and focusing on development and improvement in the future rather than looking to the past.

Goleman (2004) draws attention to the considerable skill necessary to carry out performance management effectively. He suggests managers need to become 'artful critics'. He argues that *not* being critical is very costly to the organisation in terms of effectiveness and to individuals in terms of their career development and job satisfaction. However, 'artfulness' and emotional intelligence are also necessary. So to Goleman, good appraisal consists of being specific and offering a solution, together with being present and being sensitive.

Armstrong (2006) draws attention to the potential role of performance management in developing a positive psychological contract and, citing Guest and Conway (2002), suggests that the psychological contract has a crucial effect on employee commitment and motivation. These attempts to mitigate the negative impact of power on the process, by influencing the nature of the relationship between staff and managers, points to a response to the deficiencies of individual performance management and appraisal. It lies in leadership based on personal effectiveness supported by good supervisory practice.

For you, leading appraisal, therefore, perhaps constitutes a challenge. How can you approach what is currently often a negative and unpopular event and make it positive and productive for you and your team? Appraisal is pretty much the norm now in health and social care, so a lot of time is wasted on an unproductive activity; turning it around could improve morale and make a better use of you and your team's time and skills. Improvement perhaps begins with addressing our own attitudes, approaching appraisal as an opportunity to empower rather than an unnecessary chore.

REFLECTION POINT

How do you view appraisal? What might you do to improve your practice? How does your team view appraisal? What could you do to engage your team in planning to improve appraisal?

Developing a humanistic and a democratic learning culture

Of the four learning cultures which we have suggested need to be combined to create a suitable learning culture in health and social care, the communal ones, developing a humanistic and a democratic learning culture, are the hardest to address. To help with the development of these two tough-to-achieve dimensions, we have developed a schema that adds a bit more depth on what might be the features of a democratic and humanistic learning culture (see Figure 7.2).

Accepting that team activities – such as group supervision and working with a team to improve processes and services – might be good ways to develop team culture, it is also useful to look at what contributing to team development might mean from the perspective of an individual team member wanting to play their part in developing a community of practice (see Table 7.4).

A real challenge for you as a team leader/supervisor is working with your team on these more nebulous but crucial dimensions. It can be useful to engage the team in discussing the different dimensions and exploring together the extent to which you might be seen to have a democratic and humanistic learning culture.

Developing team awareness can help create opportunities for team problem solving, which can also be very useful. Group supervision which we discussed earlier can be a good opportunity for this. Munro is encouraging a move towards group problem solving in her proposal for multi-disciplinary teams to carry out case reviews to identify successes and problems with a view to improving services (SCIE, 2012b). This raises the issue of how outward looking is your community of practice? A strong community of practice will reach out to the multi-disciplinary team and the wider organisation, in effect, welcoming them in and seeking their contribution to the communities of practice.

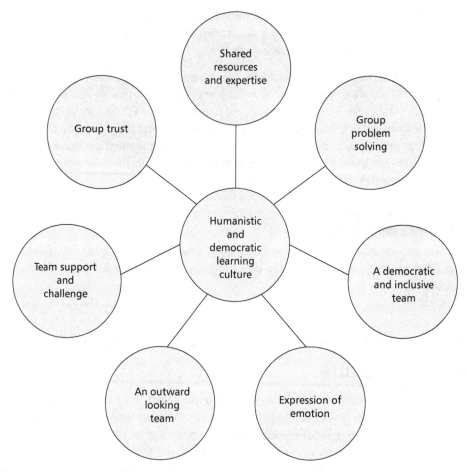

Figure 7.2 Developing a humanistic and democratic learning culture

Table 7.4 Behaviours that will support a community of practice

---

SHARED RESOURCES AND EXPERTISE
What are your areas of expertise?
How do you share your expertise with colleagues?
What are the areas of expertise held by your colleagues?
Do you make use of your colleagues' expertise?
Do you have shared team resources, e.g. books, papers, electronic resources
Do you coach and advise colleagues when they need help?

GROUP PROBLEM SOLVING
Do you share practice problems with colleagues?
Do you listen to their thoughts and suggestions?
Do you listen and share your perspectives when colleagues share their practice?
Do you contribute to more formal group problem solving and learning situations, e.g. team meetings, group supervision?
Do you share information about new policy and practices with the team?

Table 7.4 Continued

DEMOCRATIC AND INCLUSIVE

Do you have a shared team development/improvement plan?

Do you identify common quality problems in delivering services?

Are you active in working collaboratively to improve services?

Do you contribute to team decision-making and the introduction of new policies and practices?

Do you ensure all colleagues are included in team activities?

EXPRESSION OF EMOTION

Do you reflect on the feelings generated by your practice?

Do you share your feelings with colleagues?

Do you share feelings and emotional experiences from your personal life?

Do you listen and accept colleagues' expressions of feelings and emotional responses?

OUTWARD LOOKING

Do you involve people who use services in improving the service?

Do you welcome colleagues from other teams into your team and share resources?

Do you collaborate with other teams in developing and improving the service?

Do you identify and share the expertise and resources of other teams?

SUPPORT AND CHALLENGE

Do you challenge behaviours, perspectives and practices that you see as unhelpful or inappropriate?

Do you give colleagues balanced feedback?

Do you identify team members who might be excluded or marginalised and help draw them into the team?

Do you welcome and help introduce new members into the team?

Do you try to resolve conflict and find common ground and ways forward?

GROUP TRUST

Are you honest and open in the team?

Do you demonstrate that you value colleagues and their views?

Do you take opportunities to praise colleagues and give them positive feedback?

Do you share personal information with colleagues?

Do you share your values and viewpoints?

Do you initiate and contribute to team social events?

Do you support colleagues grappling with difficult situations and seek support yourself?

(Gray et al., forthcoming)

REFLECTION POINT

Does the team you supervise exhibit the behaviours in Table 7.4? What might you do to help develop a humanistic and democratic learning culture in the team?

Chapter 8
Developing supervision practice

This chapter addresses the key dimensions which should be considered in attempting to develop supervision practice. We are at something of a crossroads at the moment in terms of the future of supervision. There are important nationally driven improvement initiatives, but the best way to develop supervisory practice has not really been explored. Rather, there is a tendency to fall back on offering training as the best way forward, and whilst this might help, there are other approaches and issues that need consideration.

A crucial factor is that, whilst a lot is said about empowering professionals, it could be argued that this is being done through top-down policy initiatives and that these have little chance of success and are more likely to reinforce current organisational cultures that have been seen to disempower professional social workers. Indeed there is perhaps a danger that improving supervision becomes something of a panacea. Yet turning the managerial tide will not be easy, especially in a time of resource constraint, so in this chapter we have tried to take a broad look at developing supervisory practice which opens up some of the dimensions too often ignored and gives you the opportunity to be more considered in your approach.

This final consideration of methodology, how we approach developing supervision, is perhaps a fitting conclusion to the previous chapters which have attempted to open up the issues in a difficult and contended area of practice. And whilst it might be obvious by now, it is worth noting again that this book as a whole has been orientated towards helping you as a supervisor take responsibility for working with your team and developing your own supervisory practice. We see this as the foundation of any successful initiatives: your ownership and engagement are crucial as only you can drive improvements. You, in conjunction with your team, are also best placed to problem solve, to identify strengths, areas for improvement and priorities, and make design choices, so that supervision meets your needs.

If engaging and mobilising you as a supervisor is an important dimension, then improvement initiatives will need to reach beyond this. For instance, the research base for supervision is very limited; so developing a robust body of critical theory and well constructed research in the longer term is essential in order to provide a secure evidence base on which to evaluate personal and organisational practice. There also needs to be a focus on developing middle managers and supervising supervisors as they will be crucial factors in bringing change. So a broad approach will be necessary and we have tried to encompass that in this chapter.

Auditing practice using the Effective Supervision Unit

One of the casualties of a lack of joined up policy initiatives has been the lack of attention given to the workforce development tool produced by Skills for Care and CWDC called *Providing Effective Supervision*. This is designed to provide a model of good practice and to assist in auditing and improving supervision (SfC/CWDC, 2007). Only some employers are making use of it and there is little reference to it in the development of standards for employers by the SWRB. Accepting its limitations, which we will discuss, it does have some merit in providing a set of standards which can be used to audit practice. The standards can be used as a benchmark against which an individual supervisor or supervisee or the organisation can evaluate current practice and develop improvement plans.

As Gray *et al.* (2010a) argue, such standards can be double edged; they can provide an invaluable point of reference by which to assess your practice. However, they can appear to be definitive and scientific, which can then limit any consideration of practice outside of the parameters they inevitably set. Their usefulness is also dependent on their application; a tick box exercise will yield only partial information, but may complete the task. If, however, the standards are used to explore the strengths and weaknesses of supervision with a team in a safe and empowering framework, then meaningful conclusions can perhaps be reached, with the potential to develop an action plan for improvement. Such an approach also allows the standards themselves to be discussed and not treated as definitive.

The unit is divided into three parts called elements:

1. Implementing supervision systems and processes.

2. Developing, maintaining and reviewing effective supervisory relationships.

3. Developing, maintaining and reviewing practice and performance through supervision.

Each of these elements is broken down into detailed performance criteria so that the whole offers a valuable good practice framework.

Although the guidance for the unit states it is particularly relevant to first line managers, it seems important for any organisation to ensure that middle managers are also involved in any process that audits and reviews supervisory practices. The standards can apply equally well to middle manager supervision of first line supervisors. Indeed they perhaps need to be implemented at all levels if they are to have a lasting impact on service quality.

There are, however, problems with this approach to improving supervision. The standards perhaps deserve a round of applause as the first attempt to define good supervisory practice. From a 'hard' task focused management perspective, they provide a comprehensive set of standards. However, if we add some of the 'softer' relationship and cultural issues, there are contentions to deal with:

- practice is too complex to have a definitive statement about what is 'good';

- whilst it gives attention to relationships, it is difficult to develop meaningful 'standards' for good relationships;

- some will demand considerable cultural change and be hard to implement. For instance, giving feedback on supervision is not established practice and a challenge for everyone;

- they are very managerial and rather daunting;

- they don't address the issues of team culture and the leadership challenges of engaging supervisees and ensuring they take responsibility for their supervision; in fact they may encourage managers to take control and 'do things' to the team;

- they could just result in some centrally monitored auditing activity that doesn't really change the quality of supervision and soon runs out of steam.

CASE STUDY 8.1

I looked through the standards myself after I was introduced to them on a course. I thought there was rather a lot for the team to take on in one go so I took them to team meetings in instalments so that we discussed different aspects. We'd just got on with it up until now, not really discussed it at all – well only when it went wrong, people cancelling for instance. I started us off talking about good and bad experiences and what we expected; amazing the different things that came out. I think we have all got better at preparation, something we discussed. I hope some more will come out of it.

ACTIVITY 8.1

Using the Effective Supervision Unit as an audit tool

We have reproduced the three elements of the Effective Supervision Unit as an audit tool in Appendix 3, along with some commentary besides each performance criteria, to provide prompts for you and your team. You can use this audit tool in a number of ways:

- *complete it yourself to review your own practice;*

- *work through it and discuss it in a team meeting so everyone is aware of the standards (this may demand time in several team meetings);*

- *work with each supervisee towards some conclusions about effectiveness and action points.*

Developing followership as a goal for supervisees

There is a danger in a book like this of focusing too much on the role of the supervisor and not the role of the supervisee. As we pointed out in the Introduction, it is as relevant for supervisees as their supervisors to be actively involved in sharing and developing the practice issues explored in this book. You will also have the role of supervisee in the relationship with your manager, as well as being a supervisor. A refreshing perspective on leadership in our society is 'followership'. Followership suggests that we are much too focused on leaders and their behaviour when in fact leaders are totally dependent on followers and their supportive behaviour; so leadership is perhaps better seen as a reciprocal relationship with leaders and followers having equal responsibilities. Such an approach could be seen to counteract a tendency for us to try to constantly find solutions to social problems by finding better leaders to no effect, when the behaviour of followers is what really counts. Yet in our society, being a good leader is attractive, whilst being a good follower isn't. Accepting that this bias is caused by a capitalist society which rewards leaders as somehow superior to followers in a pro-fessionalised organisation, where professionals also have responsibility for practice, followership becomes an even more powerful perspective. For instance, we argue that supervision and practice are joint responsibilities, as are the decisions made and the supporting processes and the practice that results.

Effective supervision could therefore be as much dependent on good followership as on good leadership by supervisors. So what constitutes good followership? Yukl (2006) outlines a menu for good followership (see Table 8.1).

This is a powerful expression of how ideally a supervisee might manage their relationship with their supervisor. We perhaps need to add to it making proposals for developing the service and improving processes (including supervision).

Followership is not merely an individualised phenomenon. Many of the themes in this book can provide a useful starting point for team discussions about supervision. The team might have theories and models they can contribute. Exploring supervision as a team is a good way forward, not only to gain commitment but also because supervision is under researched and needs input from practitioners to develop good practice models.

Table 8.1 Menu for good followership

- Find out what you are expected to do.
- Take the initiative to deal with problems.
- Keep the boss informed about your decisions.
- Verify the accuracy of information you give the boss.
- Encourage the boss to provide honest feedback to you.
- Support leader efforts to make necessary changes.
- Show appreciation and provide recognition when appropriate.
- Challenge flawed plans and proposals made by leaders.
- Resist inappropriate influence attempts by the boss.
- Provide upward coaching and counselling when appropriate.

(Yukl, 2006: 136, Table 5.4)

REFLECTION POINT

Are your supervisees good followers?

What might you do to encourage good followership on their part?

How might you develop their knowledge and understanding of effective supervisory practice?

Are you a good follower in your supervision?

Resistance to improving supervisory practice

One of the standards in the Effective Supervision Unit seeks to encourage supervisors and supervisees to give each other feedback on their supervision practice as a way to improve practice. One can readily see the value of this, but it is new and challenging practice. A privilege of supervision is being let into the world of someone's practice, but such intimacy can have a downside. You not only share your supervisees' struggles and emotions; supervisors and supervisees must make themselves vulnerable if there is to be open and honest dialogue. Being judged and judging can therefore be very daunting; if, as we have suggested, personal effectiveness and 'use of self' are important features of effective supervision for both you and your supervisee, this also means your supervision practice is part of you, not a distant activity that can be viewed objectively and unemotionally. Feedback from a supervisee that is challenging and therefore useful may also be uncomfortable.

So there can be a lot invested in supervision practice and being objective about it, and perhaps receiving negative feedback is not going to be easy. We also develop habits in our supervision or perhaps practices that have proven their worth by working in the past. There is emotional comfort in routines and existing repertoires and change demands energy and discomfort.

Therefore, opening up a new culture of giving feedback is not going to be easy for anyone and supervisees may be quite clumsy at first and not do it very well. But if you go into denial, they will not attempt it again. If, however, you can be seen to welcome it and act on it, even if it is uncomfortable, a whole new world can open up.

You may, therefore, need to break the ice by suggesting what you are concerned about is developing your supervision practice and seeking feedback from them and discuss how this could best be done. Once you have a dialogue which you can build on when giving them feedback, balance the objectives to work on with recognising strengths and achievements. Also don't be too ambitious on either of your parts; stay with one or two areas for improvement.

Help from your own supervisor can make big difference in this endeavour, given how challenging this area of practice can be. Share initiatives to improve practice with them so that they can support you and, if you are stuck, seek their help. Also, whilst we have no real evidence to draw on, we get the impression that exploring and improving the quality of a supervisor's supervision doesn't appear on middle managers' agendas, despite there being good reasons for considering it to be a crucial activity.

Evaluating supervision sessions

There is great value in you and your supervisee reflecting on supervision sessions after the session, either separately or together. The Effective Supervision Unit or parts of it could be used for this purpose or you could take a more open approach. Some structure can help, though, and so we have included a structure that a supervisor could use in Appendix 3 which could also readily be used by a supervisee.

ACTIVITY *8.2*

Reflecting on supervision sessions

What do you see as the barriers to developing supervisory practice in your team?

How might you overcome them?

Review the guidelines for reflecting on a supervision session (Appendix 1) and the supervision unit audit tool (Appendix 3). How might you approach reflecting on a supervision session? What might assist your supervisee to do so?

Organisational initiatives to improve practice

A whole systems approach to improving supervision

Hawkins and Shohet (2006) draw attention to the importance of the wider organisation in bringing improvement to supervision and recent policy initiatives to improve leadership in health and social care have taken a 'whole systems approach'. Such a comprehensive approach to improving supervision would demand a planning model with several levels of activity. Accepting the limitations we have discussed, the Effective Supervision Unit standards can do a lot to support such an organisation-wide approach so that an organisational supervision planning initiative based on the SFC management and leadership development good practice model might look like Table 8.2 (SfC, 2012b: 22–3).

Table 8.2 Levels of organisational supervision planning initiative

Level	Features
Pre-qualifying	• Supervision standards integrated into assessment of students. • Supervision skills and responsibilities of supervisees taught and assessed. • Relationship with practice educator used to develop practice and introduce supervision standards.
NQSW, ASYE and probationary period	• Standards integrated into recruitment and selection of staff. • Supervision policy and supervision practice is part of the induction programme. • Supervision standards included in end of year assessment to assess supervisee.
Individual supervisee	• Supervision contract based on NQSW/ASYE and identifying areas for improvement. • Supervision objectives in personal development plan and point of reference in appraisal. • Team development/improvement plan for supervision. • Supervision practice enhanced and assessed as part of post-qualifying (PQ) training.

Table 8.2 Continued

Level	Features
Individual supervisor	• Supervision standards integrated into recruitment, selection and induction. • 360-degree feedback on supervisory practice. • Standards used to develop supervision of supervisors. • Access to a variety of on and off the job learning activities to develop supervision – shadowing, placements, coaching, mentoring, projects and action learning groups. • Integrated with general leadership and management development planning, monitoring and evaluation.
Individual middle manager	• Supervision standards integrated into recruitment, selection and induction. • 360-degree feedback on supervisory practice. • Access to a variety of on and off the job learning activities to develop their supervision of supervisees – shadowing, placements, coaching and mentoring and projects. • Standards integrated into their own supervision, development planning and appraisal. • Leading supervisory teams included in general leadership and management development opportunities for middle managers.
Senior manager and organisation	• Supervision policy. • Supervision improvement plan/strategy. • Senior manager/owner with lead responsibility. • Systems for monitoring and evaluating long-term quality improvements in supervision which reach beyond performance measures and crude auditing. • Funding streams to support development of supervision. • Senior and middle manager improvement initiatives including developing learning organisations.
Partnerships	• Development of partnerships with local training and education providers. • Development of HE partnerships to research, develop and disseminate good practice. • Creating joint learning opportunities and initiatives with other agencies such as health, education, private and voluntary agencies. • Using partnership networks as opportunities to extend on the job learning through work exchanges, shadowing, projects, placements and meetings. • Using partnerships to access specialist supervision.

We are back to the learning organisation issues, so it helps if you are part of a broader organisational-wide initiative to develop supervision. If your organisation is a learning organisation with a shared/distributed leadership approach this is likely, and you will be involved in proposing and making improvements from the beginning. However, even if you are not in a position to encourage and play a part in a wider initiative, you can still achieve a lot by developing a micro-culture within your team, as a community of practice that gives emphasis to developing the quality of supervision. This can generate tensions with the wider organisation, but there may be opportunity to mobilise some parts to help you. So if you are, in effect, the champion for developing supervision and focus on your team, still try to get support from other systems and stakeholders. So, for instance, try to engage your manager and you might well be able to influence partner organisations as well.

REFLECTION POINT

What can you do to encourage and support organisational-wide initiatives to improve supervision?

Who are the other stakeholders in your team's supervisory practice? How might you engage them so that they support you and the team in improving supervision and developing practice?

Developing supervision practice: a planned approach

We have developed a three-step approach to developing your supervision practice:

1. In Figure 8.1 we have identified some of the dimensions which need to be taken into account in analysing current practice.

2. Building on the discussions above, which draw attention to the leadership and followership issues and the psychological dimensions, a useful approach to developing your supervisory practice can be a Strengths, Weaknesses, Opportunities and Threats (SWOT) analysis (see Table 8.3). This is a useful planning tool which you may have come across that is designed to assist in developing business strategy. It lends itself well to supporting team initiatives to improve supervision as it is best completed with a team, so that they contribute to the information and analysis and own the objectives and improvement plan.

Points to remember

- The analysis is only as good as the information drawn on. For instance, your team's views on the strengths of supervision are useful, but ensure you have the evidence.

- Whilst some celebration of success is useful as well as some honest identification of problems, try to maintain a balanced view identifying strengths and weaknesses – reaching for viewpoints supported by evidence can help with this.

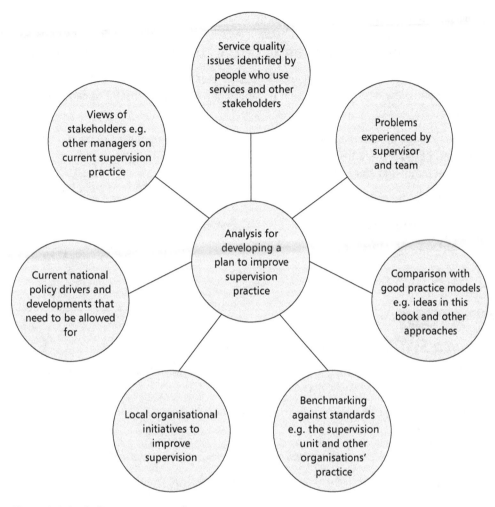

Figure 8.1 Analysing current practice

Table 8.3 SWOT analysis

STRENGTHS	WEAKNESSES
What are the strengths of our supervision that we can build on?	What are the areas where supervision is not meeting requirements or our needs?
OPPORTUNITIES	THREATS
What parts of the organisation and environment might support our plans for developing supervision and enhance our practice, e.g. training opportunities, new policy initiatives?	What are factors in our current practice which might get in the way of plans to improve supervision or could undermine practice?

- Whilst the focus can be on supervision processes, procedures and relationships, identification of common service quality problems which supervision can then focus on is also useful, e.g. focus on quality of assessments recently identified as a problem in an inspection.

- Whilst you might helpfully summarise strengths, weaknesses, opportunities and threats as bullet points, the depth of discussion is important and it can be useful to capture this as well.

- Strengths and weaknesses need to be allowed for in responding to opportunities and threats, i.e. your strengths and weaknesses can determine which opportunities and threats you can respond to and how you might best do this.

3. From the results of the SWOT:

  - build a series of objectives for improving supervision;

  - develop a plan of action;

  - monitor and review.

ACTIVITY 8.3

Using a SWOT analysis with your team

It can be helpful for you as team leader to think things through before involving the team in a SWOT analysis or team planning event.

What would you say are the strengths, weaknesses, opportunities and threats of current supervision practice in your team?

What information and perspectives are you drawing on in your analysis?

How will you approach involving your team in analysis and planning?

Inviting service users into the community of practice to improve supervision

There is an agreed need to involve service users in improving services in a planned way, shown by the centrality of partnership with service users in the PCF, and this should also include supervisory practice. However, rather than merely a planned approach, using the concept of community of practice is possible. The key question is: what role do people who use services have in a community of practice? You will have seen that in Table 7.4 on pages 110–11 we have suggested that being outward looking and welcoming are features of a healthy community of practice. This is because expertise and knowledge can be shared more widely and outside expertise and knowledge can be brought in to the community. This raises the question as to where the boundary of a community of practice lies.

Two useful takes on this are provided by the role of people who use services and customers in Total Quality Management (TQM) and therapeutic communities. In TQM, quality circles are used to ensure that not only are workers enabled as organisational problem solvers but they also embrace suppliers and, crucially, customers (Oakland, 2003). In therapeutic communities, this is perhaps taken a stage further with people who use services/patients involved in democratic communal decision-making and playing a part in the community on an everyday basis.

In TQM the reason for involving customers is that they are the real experts in what makes a good product or service and their involvement is therefore crucial. In therapeutic communities this also applies but involvement is more inclusive as the best people to offer guidance or influence others are seen to be fellow users or patients.

Another link to leadership practices is by considering the idea of 360-degree feedback; this is common in many public and private organisations, and may be a feature of your appraisal. However, service user involvement is much less common. Social Work Education has perhaps taken a lead on this and most qualifying programmes ensure that service user feedback is a part of every student's assessment. Innovative partnerships between service users and students have included attendance at specific supervision sessions where they have participated in reviewing the service they receive, and been invited to give feedback to the social work student (Fenge *et al.*, 2012).

In residential and day services it is possible to more fully involve people who use services in the community of practice; in fact they can be placed at its centre. It is harder in field services but we have suggested four strategies below which could help to develop more inclusive and service user focused supervision:

- encouraging user centred practice from your supervisees in all supervision sessions, i.e. people who use services are fully involved in assessment, agreeing their needs and managing their care plans;

- holding case planning meetings with service users or bringing them into supervision sessions so they are able to have a say about the service they are receiving;

- eliciting service user opinions at least once a year as part of the appraisal process and more regularly would improve practice;

- service development initiatives which involve people who use services in consultations may also have a focus on supervisory arrangements for staff.

We recognise that people who use services are often distanced from the supervisory relationship and may have little idea of what happens. However, this is not a reason to ignore the contribution that they could make. They may be far better tuned in than we might allow for and able to offer some valuable insights.

We also recognise that it is hard to make involvement meaningful for all parties, and some of the difficulties encountered in more general areas of practice indicate this. Both the service user and the supervisee need to feel comfortable with the process. The supervisee can be understandably nervous, and so can the service user. It will take time, careful planning and an understanding that it may not work first time. Adapting good practice guidelines as in Gray *et al.* (2010a) will help to develop a good strategy that is respectful for everyone.

REFLECTION POINT

What opportunities can you see for involving people who use services in developing supervisory practice with your team?

What difficulties might you envisage, how might these be overcome?

Communities of practice/action learning sets for supervisors

Support for supervisors in developing supervisory practice has an important part to play if attempts to improve supervision are to be successful. Hopefully a book like this helps a little, but there are a number of problems to be overcome. Supervision may not have received the attention it should have in the past, so there is arguably a shortage of expertise in organisations. Research into supervision practice has also been very limited so that there are no clear answers and no clear ideas about how best to support supervisors. De-layering in organisations, generated by funding cuts, can mean that there are not middle managers available to support supervisors.

It is worth giving some time to thinking about your support and, given the problems above, an option worth considering is establishing action/learning sets with colleagues, meeting regularly to explore and develop supervision practice and discuss problems together. If you are all based and working together, this could be seen as developing a community of practice for supervisors or as group supervision for supervisors. In any event it offers a valuable option and there are huge advantages in learning from one another and developing practice together when knowledge and support are limited.

An independent facilitator can help but a revolving chair is an alternative approach. Meetings could encompass:

- problems individuals are experiencing in supervision for exploration;

- progress on team initiatives to develop supervision;

- organisational initiatives to develop supervision and how group members could contribute;

- exploration of how individuals are developing their practice and sharing resources and opportunities;

- invitations to others with expertise or useful experiences to join and share with the group;

- a 'case review' approach – exploring together a case where supervision has broken down or failed or one where it has been successful in order to develop practice (SCIE, 2012).

Supervising supervisors

Given our discussion in the rest of this book, there is a compelling case for you as a supervisor to receive proper supervision yourself, yet our experience indicates that many supervisors are under supported; some receiving no supervision, many experiencing inadequate supervision which looks at management issues in general but doesn't support supervision practice. For instance, the help supervisors receive with handling performance problems can be very limited.

What should a supervision agenda for supervisors perhaps look like? Certainly it should be shaped by you – it should be a shared agenda. It should probably encompass:

- Case management problems.

- Individual performance management problems – not just the task issues but also the emotional impact on you.

- A review of each supervisory relationship.

- Mediation (your supervisor can play a crucial role in helping keep you informed about organisational developments and taking issues for you and your team to the wider organisation).

- Initiatives to help develop supervision practice.

- General management of the team, e.g. budget management, performance measures, training management, etc.

- Your performance management, CPD and personal development planning including developing supervision practice.

In sum, it is not that different from what you are providing for your supervisees and we would argue that someone supervising supervisors also needs much the same knowledge and skills as you do as a supervisor and that there is mirroring effect between the relationships. A supervisee carries attitudes, behaviours and emotion from practice into supervision and those experienced in their supervision into practice. A supervisor carries attitudes, behaviours and emotion from supervisory practice into their supervision and those experienced in their supervision into their supervisory practice. There is, therefore, perhaps a common agenda which generates the same dilemmas we have explored earlier in this book. For instance, how do you prevent a supervisor's supervision being dominated by case management crises and ensure it is developmental, given the pressures of practice?

It is perhaps rather sad that there has been little discussion of how the Effective Supervision Unit standards might be applied to the supervision of supervisors or the role of middle managers in developing supervision practice and what their support and developmental needs and options might be. Yet we would argue the standards are useful and readily applicable, even allowing for their limitations, and improvement initiatives for middle mangers, in tandem with supervisors and supervisees, would greatly improve outcomes.

A useful alternative to action learning sets which can assist with developing supervision practice is mentoring. (For further information, see Holroyd and Field, 2012.) This can be used to support supervision of a supervisor by their manager and has the advantage of drawing on expertise from across the organisation (Williams *et al.*, 2012). It also has the advantage of providing a neutral source of advice that can allow a more ready exploration of some of the more sensitive and emotionally demanding issues, including a supervisor's performance.

ACTIVITY *8.4*

Receiving support as a supervisor

What options are there for you to improve the support you receive as a supervisor?

What could you do to improve and support your manager's supervision of your practice?

Appendix 1

Personal reflection on a supervision session: some key questions

The full Effective Supervision Unit provides the basis for reflection on supervision practice. However, some useful quick questions to consider after a session are:

Reflecting on the management of the task

- Did you get the information you needed to prepare?
- Had your staff member prepared?
- Did you check progress on actions from the previous session?
- Did you agree an agenda and cover it?
- Did each case/item get the time it needed according to its priority?
- Did you achieve good depth of discussion in exploring each case?
- Are you both clear on actions i.e. who, what and when?
- Are there any other issues that the session didn't cover or information that you need? What will you do about this?
- Are all cases getting the attention they need?
- Did you make opportunity to reflect on and discuss learning and personal development?
- Did you give feedback on good practice and identify any practice that needed improving?
- Were key issues and decisions and actions recorded?
- Did you plan together for your next supervision session?

Reflecting on the relationship

(based on the National Occupational Standards for Counselling CLG2.1, ENTO, 2007)

- Were there any areas of conflict? Have they been resolved? How were they resolved?
- Did you leave sufficient space for your staff member's agenda and allow your staff member to contribute?

- What feelings did you experience during the sessions and what generated them?

- How do you feel at the end of the session? What might be generating those feelings?

- Are you in any ways stuck or struggling to work with this staff member? What might be causing this? What can you do?

- Did your staff member show any signs of discomfort during the session? What might have caused this?

- When did they seem engaged and positive? What might have caused this?

- What do you think your staff member might be feeling at the end of the session? What might have caused this?

- Are you developing and improving your practice as a supervisor?

- Thinking back over sessions, are there any common themes emerging that may be significant in case management, the supervisees' reactions and practices or in our relationship?

ENTO, 2007. National Occupational Standards for Counselling CLG2.1. Leicester: ENTO

Appendix 2

SCIE learning organisation audit: auditing organisational development

Please rate the following with regard to the **information systems** used within your organisation:

	Strongly agree	Agree	Not yet decided	Disagree	Strongly disagree
There are effective information systems for both internal and external communication					
The organisation makes good use of IT to improve information exchange and management					
Information is freely available					
Where possible, information is shared openly with people who use services and their carers					
Policies and procedures are meaningful and understood by all					

Please rate the following statements in terms of how they apply to the **structure** of your organisation:

	Strongly agree	Agree	Not yet decided	Disagree	Strongly disagree
Feedback and participation of people who use services and carers is actively sought					
Team working, learning and utilising all staff skills are integral to the organisation					
There is cross-organisational, collaborative and partnership working					

Please rate the following statements in terms of how far they apply to the **culture** of your organisation:

	Strongly agree	Agree	Not yet decided	Disagree	Strongly disagree
There is a system of shared beliefs, values, goals and objectives					
Development of new ideas and methods is encouraged					
An open learning environment allows the opportunity to test innovative practice					
New evidence and research are considered and incorporated into practice					
Ideas and proposals can come from any part of the organisation – not just 'top down'					
People who identify problems are not blamed					

Are the following examples of **human resource practice** present in your workplace?

	Strongly agree	Agree	Not yet decided	Disagree	Strongly disagree
There is a commitment to continuous personal/career development for all staff and by all staff					
Individual learning styles and learning needs are responded to					
A good range of formal and informal learning opportunities are open to all					
A high quality of individual supervision and support is offered					

Are the following **leadership strengths** established in the organisation you work for?

	Strongly agree	Agree	Not yet decided	Disagree	Strongly disagree
The organisation develops and improves services wherever it can					
Leaders model the openness, risk-taking and reflection necessary for learning					
Leaders ensure that the organisation has the resources and capacity to learn, change and develop					
Learning and development opportunities are linked to organisational objectives					

These questions have been adapted from the SCIE website (see: **www.scie.org.uk/ publications/learningorgs/files/key_characteristics_2.pdf**).

Appendix 3
Effective Supervision Unit audit tool

In the following table we have added a commentary to the Effective Supervision Unit audit tool which is based on the supervisee's perspective.

How could you use the audit tool to improve the quality of your practice as a supervisor?

How could you use it to improve the quality of the supervision that you receive?

Audit Tool

A strength of our current practice		Needs radical improvement		
1	2	3	4	5

1.1 Implement supervision systems and processes

Performance criteria	Commentary
a. Implement supervision in the context of organisational policies, performance management and workforce development. 1 2 3 4 5	You need to locate and familiarise yourself with your organisation's supervision, appraisal, probationary and personal development policies and procedures.
b. Develop, implement and review written agreements for supervision. 1 2 3 4 5	It is usual to have a supervision contract that summarises arrangements and responsibilities. They can be rudimentary, simply stating frequency, length and who has responsibility for setting them up. More complex contracts cover cancellation procedures, preparation and so on. Others may set ground rules for the relationship and identify such things as areas of interest or for personal development.
c. Ensure supervision records and agreed decisions are accurate and completed promptly. 1 2 3 4 5	You need to keep a record, at the very least, of decisions made in supervision and whoever has responsibility for recording them will need them to be agreed and signed off. Usually it is the supervisor's responsibility, but you should have a signed copy for your records or at least access to them.

Performance criteria	Commentary
d. Enable workers to reflect on supervision issues and act on outcomes. 1 2 3 4 5	Your supervisor/s should encourage and give you space to reflect on your practice and identify your strengths, weaknesses and development needs and review your actions and care plans.
e. Monitor and review own supervision practice and learning, reflecting on the processes and implement improvements to supervision. 1 2 3 4 5	There should be opportunity for you to comment on the quality of the supervision you have received.
f. Identify wider issues and raise them appropriately in the organisation and with other stakeholders. 1 2 3 4 5	Your manager or supervisor should act as a broker identifying with you practice issues that need to be picked up on in the organisation more widely, so that the quality of services can be improved.
g. Enable access to specialist supervision, support, advice or consultation as required. Specialist supervision can include peer, therapeutic or clinical supervision. 1 2 3 4 5	Specialist supervision can be an excellent way to develop your practice and can also be essential in some roles and situations which demand more support that your manager or usual supervisor/s can provide.

1.2 Develop, maintain and review effective supervision relationships

Performance criteria	Commentary
a. Create a positive environment for workers to develop and review their practice. 1 2 3 4 5	Supervision should challenge your practice but it should be a positive encounter which you value and where challenge is matched with encouragement and support. You should be encouraged to take responsibility and take control in reviewing and evaluating your practice.
b. Clarify boundaries and expectations of supervision, including confidentiality. 1 2 3 4 5	It pays to review your previous experiences of supervision and what works or doesn't work for you. Good supervision contracts will cover these broader issues as well as clarifying confidentiality and what are (or not) suitable matters for supervision.

Performance criteria	Commentary
c. Ensure relationships are conducted in an open and accountable way. 1 2 3 4 5	Both you and your supervisor/s are accountable for your practice so the relationship must be strong enough for you to share the details of your practice, including problems you are experiencing. Hidden practice can be dangerous practice.
d. Help workers to identify and overcome blocks to performance, such as work conflicts and other pressures. 1 2 3 4 5	Effective practice is not just down to you. Others can influence your effectiveness in a positive fashion, as well as negatively. Your supervisor/s should also be able to help with these broader issues.
e. Assist workers to understand the emotional impact of their work and seek appropriate specialist support if needed. 1 2 3 4 5	It is a tough job – one that can affect us all deeply. The emotion of your work needs to be on the agenda for the sake of your own health, but also because it can impact on your practice. Some people who use services can be manipulative or frightening – openness about their impact on you will help ensure your practice is purposeful and objective.
f. Ensure the **duty of care** is met for the wellbeing of workers. 1 2 3 4 5	Your employer has responsibility for your health and safety including safe working arrangements outside of the office, stress and workload balance.
g. Recognise diversity and demonstrate **anti-discriminatory practice** in the supervision relationship. 1 2 3 4 5	Supervision should respond to your individual needs and actively seek not to discriminate against you.
h. Give and receive constructive **feedback** on the supervisory relationship and supervision practice. 1 2 3 4 5	Both you and your supervisor/s need to reflect on and discuss the quality of your supervision and aim to improve it over time.
i. Audit and develop own skills and knowledge to supervise workers, including those from other disciplines when required. 1 2 3 4 5	Your manager should be seeking to develop their skills as a supervisor. You can help them do this by giving them positive and constructive feedback, identifying areas where supervision can be improved. Having good supervisory practice on the agenda is also useful as the supervision of others will become one of your responsibilities as your career progresses.

1.3 Develop, maintain and review practice and performance through supervision

Performance criteria	Commentary
a. Ensure workloads are effectively allocated, managed and reviewed. 1 2 3 4 5	It is very difficult to come up with a definitive workload management system that determines fair workloads for all, as your work will be too complex and variable to be easily categorised and measured. Good dialogue that regularly addresses what you are being allocated, how this is done, and whether it is manageable, is essential.
b. Monitor and enable workers' competence to assess, plan, implement and review their work. 1 2 3 4 5	Your performance as a case manager should be evaluated and there should be opportunities for you to develop and improve your practice.
c. Ensure supervisor and workers are clear about accountability and the limits of their individual and organisational authority and duties. 1 2 3 4 5	Induction and supervision are the best places to clarify any areas of confusion that can arise. Job descriptions and procedures are often not definitive – discussion works.
d. Ensure workers understand and demonstrate **anti-discriminatory practice**. 1 2 3 4 5	Your qualifying course will have given a lot of attention to this topic, but do not let it drift – make it an explicit feature of your supervision agenda.
e. Ensure work with **people who use services** is outcomes-focused and that their views are taken account of in service design and delivery. 1 2 3 4 5	Work with individuals needs to be achieving outcomes agreed with them. Supervision also needs to address the broader development of services and service quality. People who use services can be involved in this.
f. Identify risks to users of services and workers and take appropriate action. 1 2 3 4 5	Risks need to be clearly identified, methodically assessed and actions agreed to manage them effectively. Any assessment and agreed plans should be recorded.
g. Obtain and give timely feedback on workers' practice, including feedback from people who use services. 1 2 3 4 5	Both you and your supervisor have a responsibility to evaluate your practice and improve it. Actively seeking feedback on your performance (especially from people who use services and carers) and discussing and acting on it is a joint responsibility.

Performance criteria	Commentary
h. Identify learning needs and integrate them within development plans. 1 2 3 4 5	It is important that you are clear about what areas of your practice you want to develop. Make sure your learning objectives and development plans are focused on these needs.
i. Create opportunities for learning and development. 1 2 3 4 5	You should be offered and take opportunity to make use of a range of on and off the job development opportunities. Their effectiveness in meeting your needs should be evaluated.
j. Assess and review performance, challenge poor practice and ensure improvements in standards. 1 2 3 4 5	Supervision should encompass appraisal. Your performance should be evaluated jointly against agreed standards on the basis of readily identified evidence. The evaluation and agreed improvement plans should be recorded together with any differences of opinion.
k. Enable multi-disciplinary, integrated and collaborative working as appropriate. 1 2 3 4 5	This is essential to service quality and demands regular review and evaluation. Many quality problems originate here and many quality improvements lie with more effective multi-agency and collaborative working.

Appendix 4
Well-formed outcome template

State your outcome in the positive. What do you want to achieve and why is it really important? Make it as detailed as possible.

What is the context in which it will be achieved? When, where, who with, etc.?

Evidence: How will you know when you have succeeded (or are on the right track)? What will you see, hear and feel when you achieve it? (using your imagination)

Resources: What are the internal (to you) and external resources you need to achieve your outcome? They need to be in your control. If not then you need to think about how you might gain control, or consider other resources, or change the outcome.

How does this fit with the wider system? Who or what 'in the system' might be affected by this change positively and negatively? Does it fit with your/others' values? What barriers might you face and how will you overcome them?

What is good about the present situation that might cause resistance to change? (Secondary Gain)

Is the reward of achieving this outcome big enough to compensate you for the loss of how things are now – if not, what would it take for the new outcome to be really compelling?

Desirability check. Having got this far – do you really want this? What else could you add to this plan to make it more desirable?

What is your first step? What specifically will you do? What is the action you will **commit** to?

Bibliography

Adair, J. (1983) *Effective Leadership.* London: Pan.

Alban-Metcalfe, J. and Alimo-Metcalfe, B. (2009) Engaging leadership part one: competencies are like Brighton Pier. *International Journal of Leadership in Public Services,* 5(1): 10–18.

Alimo-Metcalfe, B. and Alban-Metcalfe, R. (2001) The development of a new transformational leadership questionnaire. *Journal of Occupational and Organisational Psychology,* 74: 1–27.

Alimo-Metcalfe, B., Alban-Metcalfe, J., Bradley, M., Mariathasan, J. and Samele, C. (2008) The impact of engaging leadership on performance, attitudes to work and wellbeing at work: a longitudinal study. *Journal of Health Organisation & Management,* 22(6): 586–98.

Armstrong, M. (2006) *Performance Management: Key Strategies and Practical Guidelines.* London: Kogan Page.

Baginsky, M., Moriarty, J., Manthorpe, J., Stevens, M., MacInnes, T. and Nagendran, T. (2010) Social workers' workload survey: messages from the frontline. London: Social Work Taskforce. Available from: www.kcl.ac.uk/sspp/departments/sshm/scwru/pubs/2010/baginskyetal2010social.pdf

Bass, B.M. (1985) *Leadership and Performance beyond Expectations.* New York: Free Press.

Beresford, P. (2003) *It's Our Lives: A Short Theory of Knowledge, Distance and Experience.* London: Citizen Press.

Beresford, P. and Croft, S. (2002) Involving service users in management: citizenship, access and support, in Reynolds, J., Henderson, J., Seden, J., Charlesworth, L. and Bullman, A. (eds) *The Managing Care Reader.* London: Routledge.

Brown, A. and Bourne, I. (1996) *The Social Work Supervisor.* Buckingham: OUP.

Brown, K., Keen, S. and Young, N. (2005) *Making it Work.* Birmingham: Learn to Care.

Burgess R. (2005) A model for enhancing individual and organisational learning of emotional intelligence: the drama and winner's triangles. *Social Work Education: The International Journal,* 24(1): 97–112.

Carroll, M. (2010) Supervision: critical reflection for transformational learning (part 2). *The Clinical Supervisor,* 29: 1–19.

Carroll, M. and Gilbert, M. (2005) *On Becoming a Supervisee: Creating Learning Partnerships.* London: Vulcani Press.

Charvet, S. (1997) *Words that Change Minds.* Iowa: Kendall/Hunt.

Collins, S. (2007) Statutory social workers: stress, job satisfaction, coping, social support and individual differences. *British Journal of Social Work,* 38(6): 1173–93.

Covey, S. (2004) *The 7 Habits of Highly Effective People.* New York: Simon Schuster.

Davys, A. and Beddoe, L. (2010) *Best Practice in Supervision.* London: Jessica Kingsley.

De Janasz, A., Dowd, K. and Schneider, B. (2011) *Interpersonal Skills in Organizations*, 4th edn. New York: McGraw-Hill.

Dixon, J. and Dogan, R. (2003) *The Contending Perspectives on Public Management: A Philosophical Investigation*. The Governance Network, Plymouth Business School, University of Plymouth, UK. Available from: www.research.plymouth.ac.uk/govern/for%20approaches%20to%20research.htm#SOCIAL THEORY AND GOVERNANCE

Doherty, C. and Thompson, J. (2007) *Leadership.* London: Hodder Education.

ENTO (2007) *National Occupational Standards for Counselling.* Available from: www.ento.co.uk/standards/counselling

Fenge, L., Howe, K., Hughes, M. and Thomas, G. (2012) *The Social Work Portfolio: A Guide for Students*. London: Open University Press.

Fook, J. and Gardner, F. (2007) *Practising Critical Reflection: A Resource Handbook*. Maidenhead: OUP.

Gibbs, G. (1988) *Learning by Doing: A Guide to Teaching and Learning Methods*. Oxford: Oxford Brookes University.

Goleman, D. (1996) *Emotional Intelligence*. London: Bloomsbury.

Goleman, D. (1998) *Working with Emotional Intelligence*. London: Bloomsbury.

Goleman, D. (2004) What makes a good leader? *Harvard Business Review*, 82(1): 82–91.

Gould, N. and Baldwin, M. (2004) *Social Work, Critical Reflection and the Learning Organisation*. Aldershot: Ashgate.

Govier, I. and Nash, S. (2009) Examining transformational approaches to effective leadership in healthcare settings. *Nursing Times*, 105(18): 24–7.

Graen, G. and Cashman, J.F. (1975) A role making model of leadership in formal organisations: a developmental approach. In Hunt, J.G. and Larson, L.L. (eds) *Leadership Frontiers.* Kent, OH: Kent State University Press.

Gray, I., Parker, J. and Immins, T. (2008) Leading communities of practice in social work. Groupwork or management? *Groupwork Journal*, special issue, *Groupwork and Management*, ed. Ward, D., 18(2): 26–41.

Gray, I., Field, R. and Brown, K. (2010a) *Effective Leadership, Management and Supervision in Health and Social Care*. Exeter: Learning Matters.

Gray, I., Parker, J., Rutter, L. and Williams, S. (2010b) Developing communities of practice: a strategy for effective leadership, management and supervision in social work. *Social Work & Social Sciences Review*, 14(1): 27–46.

Gray, I., Parker, J., Rutter, L. and Williams, S. (forthcoming) Empowering professionals: reaching beyond managerialism and developing communities of practice.

Gross, R. (1996) *The Science of Mind and Behaviour*, 3rd edn. London: Hodder and Stoughton.

Harris, A. (2004) *Distributed Leadership and School Improvement*. Available from: www.scribd.com/doc/3369168/distributed-leadership-harris

Harrison, K. and Ruch, G. (2007) Social work and the use of self: on becoming a social worker. In Lymbery, M. and Postle, K. (eds) *Social Work: A Companion to Learning*. London: Sage.

Hawkins, P. and Shohet, R. (2006) *Supervision in the Helping Professions*, 3rd edn. Maidenhead: OUP.

Hawthorne, L. (1975) Games supervisors play. *Social Work*, 20: 179–83.

Health and Care Professions Council (HCPC) (2012) *Continuing Professional Development and Your Registration*. Available from: www.hcpc-uk.org

Heifetz, R.A. (1994) *Leadership without Easy Answers*. Cambridge, MA: Harvard University Press.

Henwood, S. and Lister, J. (2007) *NLP and Coaching for Health Care Professionals*. Chichester: Wiley.

Heron, J. (2001) *Co-operative Inquiry: Research into the Human Condition*. London: Sage.

Hersey, P. and Blanchard, K.H. (1993) *Management of Organisational Behaviour: Utilising Human Resources*, 6th edn. London: Prentice Hall.

Hess, A.K. (ed) (1980) *Psychotherapy Supervision: Theory, Research and Practice*. New York: Wiley.

Holroyd, J. (2012) *Improving Personal and Organisational Performance in Social Work*. London: Sage/Learning Matters.

Holroyd, J. and Field, R. (2012) *Performance Coaching Skills for Social Work*. London: Sage/Learning Matters.

Honey, P. and Mumford, A. (1986) *Using Your Learning Styles*. Maidenhead: Honey Publishers.

Huczynski, A. and Buchanan, D. (2007) *Organisational Behaviour: An Introductory Text*, 4th edn. Prentice Hall: London.

Hughes, L. and Pengelly, P. (1997) *Staff Supervision in a Turbulent Environment*. London: Jessica Kingsley.

Huxley, A. (2004) *Point Counter Point*. London: Random House.

Jack, G. and Donnellan, H. (2010) Recognising the person within the developing professional: tracking the early careers of newly qualified child care social workers in three local authorities in England. *Social Work Education*, 29(3): 305–18.

Johns, C. and Graham, J. (1996) Using a reflective model of nursing and guided reflection. *Nursing Standard*, 11(2): 34–8.

Johnson, B. (1996) *Polarity Management: Identifying and Managing Unsolvable Problems*. Amherst, MA: HRD Press.

Kadushin, A. (2002) *Supervision in Social Work*. Columbia Press: New York.

Kadushin, A. and Kadushin, G. (1997) *The Social Work Interview: A Guide for Human Service Professionals*. New York: Columbia Press.

Karpman, S. (2007) The New Drama Triangles. United States of America Transactional Analysis Association/International Transactional Analysis Association conference lecture. Available from: www.karpmandrama triangle.com/

Kinman, G. and Grant, L. (2011) Exploring stress resilience in trainee social workers: the role of emotional and social competence. *British Journal of Social Work*, 41: 261–75.

Knight, S. (2009) *NLP at Work*. London: Nicholas Brearley.

Kobasa, S. (1979) Stressful life events, personality, and health: an inquiry into hardiness. *Journal of Personality and Social Psychology*, 37: 1–11.

Kolb, D. (1984) *Experiential Learning as a Source of Learning and Development*. London: Prentice Hall.

Laming, H. (2003) *The Victoria Climbié Inquiry Report of an Inquiry by Lord Laming*. London: DoH.

Laming, H. (2009) *The Protection of Children in England: A Progress Report*. London: Stationery Office.

Loganbill, C., Hardy, E. and Delworth, U. (1982) Supervision: A conceptual model. *The Counselling Psychologist*, 10(1): 3–42.

McGregor, D. (1957) An uneasy look at performance appraisal. *Harvard Business Review*, May–June: 89–94.

Maddi, S., Kahn, S. and Maddi, K. (1998) The effectiveness of hardiness training. *Consulting Psychology Journal: Practice and Research*, 50(2): 78–86.

Miller, L. (2012) *Counselling Skills for Social Work*. London: Sage.

Mills, H. and Domeck, M. (2005) *Resilience*. Available from: www.mentalhelp.net/poc/view_doc.php?type= doc&id=5779&cn=298

Mor Barak, M., Travis, D., Pyun, H. and Bin, X. (2009) The impact of supervision on worker outcomes: a meta analysis. *Social Services Review*, 83(1): 3–32.

Morgan, G. (2006) *Images of Organisation*. London: Sage.

Morrison, T. (2005) *Supervision in Social Care*. London: Pavilion.

Morrison, T. (2007) Emotional intelligence, emotions and social work: context, characteristics, complications and contribution. *British Journal of Social Work*, (37)2: 245–63.

Mullins, L.J. (2007) *Management and Organisational Behaviour*. Harlow: Pearson.

Munro, E. (2011a) *The Munro Review of Child Protection: Interim Report: the Child's Journey*. London: Department for Education.

Munro, E. (2011b) *The Munro Review of Child Protection: Final Report. A Child-Centred System*. London: Department for Education.

O'Connor, J. (2001) *NLP Workbook*. London: Thorsons.

Oakland, J.S. (2003) *Total Quality Management: Text with Cases*, 3rd edn. London: Heinemann.

Noble, C. and Irwin, J. (2009) Social work supervision: an exploration of the current challenges in a rapidly changing social, economic and political environment. *Journal of Social Work*, 9(3): 345–58.

Phillipson, J. (2002) Supervision and being supervised, in Adams, R., Dominelli, L. and Payne, M. (eds) *Critical Practice in Social Work*. Basingstoke: Palgrave Macmillan.

Proctor, B. (2000) *Group Supervision: A Guide to Creative Practice*. London: Sage.

Raven, Bertram H. (1992) A power/interaction model of interpersonal influence: French and Raven thirty years later. *Journal of Social Behaviour and Personality*, 7(2): 217–44.

Rosenberg, M. (2003) *Nonviolent Communication*. Encinitas, CA: PuddleDancer Press.

SCIE (2004) *Learning Organisations: A Self Assessment Resource Pack*. Social Care Institute for Excellence.

SCIE (2012a) *At a Glance 01: Learning Together to Safeguard Children: A 'Systems' Model for Case Reviews*. Available from: www.scie.org.uk/publications/ataglance/ataglance01.asp

SCIE (2012b) *Dignity in Care: Stand Up for Dignity: Whistleblowing.* Available from: www.scie.org.uk/ publications/guides/guide15/standupfordignity/whistleblowing/index.asp

Seden, J. (2005) *Counselling Skills in Social Work Practice.* Maidenhead: OUP.

Senge, P.M. (1990) *The Fifth Discipline: The Art and Practice of the Learning Organisation.* London: Random House.

SfC/CWDC (2007) *Providing Effective Supervision.* Leeds: SfC. Available from: www.skillsforcare.org.uk/files/ Effective%20Supervision%20unit.pdf

Skills for Care (2012a) *Providing Effective Supervision.* Skills for Care. Available from: http://www.skillsforcare. org.uk/developing_skills/leadership_and_management/providing_effective_supervision.aspx

Skills for Care (2012b) *Leadership and Management Strategy.* Leeds: SfC. Available from: www.skillsfor care.org.uk/developing_skills/leadership_and_management/leadership_and_management_strategy.aspx

Social Work Taskforce (2009) *Building a Safe and Confident Future: Final Report of the Social Work Taskforce.* Available from: www.education.gov.uk/publications/standard/publicationdetail/page1/ DCSF-01114-2009

SWRB (2010) *Building a Safe and Confident Future: One Year On.* London: Social Work Reform Board. Available from: www.education.gov.uk/swrb

SWRB (2011) *Standards for Employers and Supervision Framework Statement [Online].* Available from: www.education.gov.uk/swrb/social/a0074240/professional-standards-for-social-workers-in-england

SWRB (2012) *Reform Board Guidance: Introduction to the ASYE May 2012.* Available from: www.skillsforcare. org.uk/asye/

Taylor, W. (2007) 5th stage of reflective competence. Available from: www.businessballs.com/conscious competencelearningmodel.htm

Thompson, N. and Gilbert, P. (2011) *Supervision Skills: A Learning and Development Manual.* Lyme Regis: Russell House Printing.

Tsui, M. (2005) *Social Work Supervision: Contexts and Concepts.* Thousand Oaks, CA: Sage.

Tuckman, B.W. (1965) Developmental sequence in small groups. *Psychological Bulletin*, 63: 384–99.

Walker, J., Crawford, K. and Parker, J. (2008) *Practice Education in Social Work: A Handbook for Practice Teachers, Assessors and Educators.* Exeter: Learning Matters.

Wenger, E. (1998) *Communities of Practice: Learning, Meaning and Identity.* Cambridge: Cambridge University Press.

Wenger, E. (2006) *Communities of Practice: A Brief Introduction.* Available from: www.ewenger.com/theory/ index.htm

Williams, S. and Rutter, L. (2010) *The Practice Educator's Handbook.* Exeter: Learning Matters.

Williams, S., Rutter, L. and Gray, I. (2012) *Promoting Individual and Organisational Learning in Social Work.* London: Sage/Learning Matters.

Yukl, G. (2006) *Leadership in Organisations*, 6th edn. New Jersey: Pearson Prentice Hall.

Index

CPSIA information can be obtained
at www.ICGtesting.com
Printed in the USA
BVHW050055090121
597004BV00005B/84